The SYSTEM BUILDER

By
XUAN NGUYEN

Edited by
NICK NGUYEN

Second Edition
X PRESS, Alviso, California

CONTENTS

Building

Meetings and Events

Mission and Crusade

Team Building

Winning

DISCLAIMER

This book is intended for internal use only, not for public distribution. All rights reserved. No part of this book may be reproduced in any form, except for training purposes.

This training manual is made available to our team for education and training purposes only.

Illustrations in the manual of how recruiting others to join our organization can affect commissions of members are not a representation of past or projected future earnings of the members.

No statement, illustration, graph, or other representation in the training manual is intended to form a contractual agreement or to modify or to supplement any existing contractual agreement between the company, the author, and the members.

The System Builder is intended as a guide to help an agent through the process of building a sales organization. Only licensed individuals may speak about products and services offered.

The Personal Financial Strategy is a customized suitability and needs analysis. The analysis is based upon information obtained from sources believed to be reliable and accurate.

While many people have experienced successful careers, this book represents individual member experiences. As each individual differs, so are his/her specific results. Work ethic patterns, activity levels, and dedication all play significant roles in determining the outcome that one may achieve and in his/her ability to control his/her destiny on an ongoing basis. This statement is not intended to nor does it represent that any current member's individual results are representative of what all participants achieve when following the information contained in this book.

Only licensed individuals may speak about products and services offered. Sales are made based on the needs, product suitability, and affordability of the clients.

Members are not required to purchase any products or services of any kind in exchange for becoming or remaining a member. Sales are made based on the needs of, and product suitability and affordability of, the client.

The author and publisher shall have neither liability nor responsibility to any person or entity with respect to any loss or damage caused, or alleged to have been caused, directly or indirectly, by the information contained in this book.

This book is sold with the understanding that the publisher and author are not engaged in rendering legal, accounting, or other professional advice or services.

PREFACE

I T MAY SOUND STRANGE, but even though I grew up in the business, I never really knew what my parents did, and honestly, I never cared to know.

I thought the people in the business were a bunch of weirdos. These people worked on Friday nights and Saturday mornings. They had to be crazy. And at conventions, people who looked like adults danced on chairs, wore the same shirt three days in a row, and shouted like sea lions, "Ooi! Ooi! Ooi!" Weird is an understatement.

So when my parents asked me to take pictures at the annual convention, I came into the event as a skeptical photographer. But I left a true believer.

What I saw amazed me. I saw doctors, lawyers, and engineers abandon their status and security for a dream and a mission. I saw women, minorities, and immigrants leading the doctors, lawyers, and engineers. I saw equality, empowerment, and a passion for a meaningful cause. I saw a business of people helping people. And I too wanted to lend a helping hand.

When the convention was over, I found myself not wanting it to end. I asked my parents when the next convention would take place. They told me March. I'd have to wait two months!

Then it hit me. People are willing to give up their weekends, spend their hard-earned money, and fly across the country to learn how to be successful in this business. "They need this information badly," I thought, "and they need it all the time, especially new people joining the business everyday."

With that in mind, I proposed that my dad gather all of his knowledge and experience into a book, so that anybody, even the newest person, could shorten their learning curve and start building their business as fast as possible.

My dad thought it was great idea. In fact, he told me that for a long time he had wanted to write a book about how to build a successful business through the system.

Due to space constraints, it was impossible for us to cover every topic of this business. But we tried our best to include the issues most relevant to the entre-preneurs who are out in the field making a difference for families and building their businesses every day. We also tried to cater to our diverse audience by switching between the masculine and feminine gen-ders when referring to a third person because, as the saying goes, "This company is run by women."

In this second edition, we updated this book to account for the changes and improvements to the system over the last 2 years with materials collected from meetings, conventions, and trainings in the U.S., Canada and Asia. While some chapters were deleted and others added, the purpose remained the same—to keep it simple—so that the team can continue to build a new generation of System Builders.

In concert with the spirit of the team, the creation of this book was a team effort. Many thanks to everyone in the team and the home office for their contributions and feedback.

Nick Nguyen
Editor

INTRODUCTION

IT IS A DREAM to have another book about our business. For the past several years in this wonderful business, we have been lucky to have all of our brochures, presentations, tapes, and training manuals prepared by the company. These materials enable us to grow and build our businesses.

As much help as these materials provide, it is still just a beginning. There is a tremendous, insatiable need for more information, considering all the thousands of new team members attending our meetings and conventions to learn, to know, and to succeed.

While writing this book, I reviewed the notes taken over the years by our builders. I was in awe of the golden nuggets left idle in these notebooks. Inside, there were great ideas, quotes, and stories delivered by many speakers, including myself, that need to be shared.

Since this book is a collection of these notes, this book is meant to complement—not replace—the current treasury of materials provided by our company. In fact, it is meant to enhance these materials and the system training that we have benefited from over the years and that have built this company to be one of the greatest success stories in this industry.

My career was shaped and influenced by perhaps the best system builders in our industry. The writing of this book is therefore a celebration as well as an appreciation of the great leaders and builders from whom we have all benefited.

On this wonderful journey, it is the team to whom I devote my life. I wonder sometimes how lucky I am to be able to associate myself with the best people on the planet. They not only make up one of the best teams in the industry, but they also set a prime example of courage, sacrifice, and people helping and caring for each other. This is a book of our team, by our team, and for our team. You are my heroes.

It is also very rewarding for me to have Nick contribute to this work. It is a dream of businesspeople around the world to have their family involved in the business.

We kept this book simple, as is the nature of the system builder. For those system builders who have committed your life to this wonderful journey, I am so excited about our future together. You are definitely the right people, at the right place, at the right time, doing the right thing—building a system that will change the world.

Your teammate,

XUAN NGUYEN
System Builder

THE SYSTEM FLOW
The MD Factory

"DO IT RIGHT"

MD TRAINEE

"DO IT WITH PRIDE"

SUBMIT U-4 (CANADA-LLQP)

"People Gathering"

QUALIFY FOR UPSTART SCHOOL IN THE FIRST 10 DAYS

GO OUT IN THE FIELD TO:

1. DEVELOP A PROSPECT LIST
2. MATCH-UP FOR FIELD RECRUITING (BMP+BPM)
3. FINALIZE YOUR PERSONAL FINANCIAL STRATEGY[2]

MD CLUB

"The Big Push"

RECRUIT 3
QUALIFY FOR MD CLUB

BUILD:

LEVEL 1: 1 MD CLUB LEG
LEVEL 2: 2 MD CLUB LEGS
LEVEL 3: 3 MD CLUB LEGS

MD SCHOOL

"The Baseshop Building Machine"

QUALIFY FOR MD

BUILD A LARGE BASE WITH 10, 15 AND 20 MD CLUBS

MD FACTORY

"The Hierarchy/Outlets Building Machine"

QUALIFY FOR EXECLUB
3 DIRECT MDs

EXECLUB MEMBER
BE COACHED BY SYSTEM BUILDERS TO BECOME CEO-MD AND BUILD A LARGE TEAM OF MDs

THE System Flow

If you want
one year of prosperity,
Grow grain.

If you want
ten years of prosperity,
Grow trees.

If you want
one hundred years of prosperity,
Grow people.

— CHINESE PROVERB

THE IMPORTANCE OF THE SYSTEM

*"If you want to be big,
you need to have a system."*

YOU ONLY NEED A SYSTEM IF YOU WANT TO BE BIG

If you want to do it small, you don't need a system.
If you want to sell all by yourself, who cares about a
system? But if you want something to duplicate and
multiply, if you want something somebody can follow,
not just you, then you need to have a system.

If you open one restaurant, you don't need a system.
But if you want to open 10 restaurants, then you got
to have a system. If you want to build thousands, you
got to be a system builder.

Unfortunately, a large number of people don't see
themselves being big. Hence, they hardly pay any
attention to a system.

BUILDERS LOVE THE SYSTEM

It's clear that great builders of any kind—great coach-
es, great entrepreneurs, great engineers, great
schools, great companies, great governments—all rely
heavily on a workable, predictable system.

GREAT ACHIEVEMENT SHOULD BE SYSTEM-DRIVEN RATHER THAN PERSONALITY-DRIVEN

Small minds pay attention to personal skills and techniques. Great minds pay attention to the system.

*"Would you rather be a 5-star chef or
the founder of McDonald's?"*

If you want to be big, you don't want a talented person in your team. You want a system builder.

1. THE SYSTEM BUILDER

The ultimate entrepreneur. Your main purpose is to build a large team and a big business, and you must build it through the system.

2. IT'S TOUGH TO BUILD THE SYSTEM

Like a railroad track, it's a pain to build the track. But when it's done, it's easy to run on. Likewise, it's hard to set up a system in your hierarchy, but when it's set, the team can grow bigger, faster. Building a team that follows the system takes tremendous discipline and sacrifice.

3. FOLLOW THE SYSTEM

You must master the system and follow the system religiously. If you want your team to copy you, you can't follow it once in a while. You must do it all the time.

*"You must create a culture of discipline
to follow the system."*

4. A SYSTEM CREATES DUPLICATION AND MULTIPLICATION

If your first generation duplicates you, your second generation will duplicate your first, and your third will duplicate your second, and on and on. That is duplication and multiplication.

"Systematize to multiply!"

5. YOUR HIGHWAY TO SUCCESS

The system shows you step-by-step exactly what you need to do to arrive to your destination. Building without a system is like driving a car without a map or directions.

6. WITHOUT THE SYSTEM

- ◆ Confusion
- ◆ Frustration
- ◆ Chaos
- ◆ Internal Conflict
- ◆ Uncoachability
- ◆ Unteachability
- ◆ Discouragement
- ◆ Quitting

7. SUBMISSION TO THE SYSTEM

The system is the product of thousands of people's efforts, many years of accumulated experience, and a few million mistakes. It has consistently been proven to be effective and has produced great success for many builders. Of course, no system is perfect—especially a system that intends to build people.

Don't try to change the system until you've understood and mastered it. That's like buying a McDonald's and tailoring it to your own tastes and style. Everything we do, the way we build—there is a reason behind it. Be a student of the business.

"You run the system.
The system runs your business."

THE SYSTEM FLOW

"A simple solution for building a big business."

- A Powerful Growth Machine
- A Clear Focus System
- A Plan to Simplify and Multiply
- A Vast New Prospect Market
- An Explosion of Presentations and Production
- Predictable and Duplicatable
- Lowers Barriers to All Builders
- Easy to Monitor
- Goal Driven / Clear Aim for Next Step
- Wide - Deep - Geometric Growth
- A Fast, Efficient Way to Build a Big Base
- Train More Trainers
- Creates Urgency and MoZone
- Mobilizes Old and New Builders
- Fosters Teamwork
- Increases Taprooting
- Liberates Builders for Expansion
- And More...

"The more you do,
the more you understand,
the more you love it."

MD

"You must try to qualify for MD
in 90 days."

All good things come with being a Marketing Director.

MD: THE ULTIMATE POSITION

▪ **You achieve the highest reward and compensation.**
You also have the most accountability and responsibility, like every leader and builder in the system.

▪ **You run your own baseshop, your own business.**
You're breaking away from your upline's baseshop.

▪ **Great income potential.** Build a big base.

▪ **Great security.** The more MDs you build, the more secure your future income will be.

You must be a MD first and duplicate the process to build a MD Factory.

"MD is the final product of our system.
Thus either you're a MD or you're a MD to be."

FOCUS ON MD

MD is your business. MD is your outlet. Your total focus is to identify, build and lead a large team of MDs. Your daily activities should comprise of anything that helps you to build new MDs. There will be big and small MDs, but those who have more MDs will be more successful.

Everyone must know the MD Guidelines.

Everyone must have the MD Checklist and know where they stand.

Keep it simple. Anyone who is serious about the business must get their license, qualify for MD Club, then qualify for MD as soon as possible.

> **Three Simple Steps to MD:**
>
> 1. SUBMIT U-4
>   (LLQP IN CANADA)
>
> 2. MD CLUB
>
> 3. MD

If you have a chance to build outlets like McDonald's, the question is how many can you build, how fast can you build them, and how many cities you should build in?

7 STEP DUPLICATION

"7 & 7: Complete the 7 Steps in 7 Days."

1. **Submit U-4**

2. **Meet the Spouse**

3. **Prospect List**

4. **Field Presentation BMP**

5. **Personal Financial Strategy**

6. **Recruit 3 Direct**

7. **Duplication**

"The perfect copy machine."

"DO IT RIGHT"

MD TRAINEE

"DO IT WITH PRIDE"

SUBMIT U-4 (CANADA-LLQP)

"People Gathering"

QUALIFY FOR UPSTART SCHOOL IN THE FIRST 10 DAYS

GO OUT <u>IN THE FIELD</u> TO:

1 *DEVELOP A PROSPECT LIST*

2 MATCH-UP FOR FIELD RECRUITING (BMP+BPM)

3 FINALIZE YOUR PERSONAL FINANCIAL STRATEGY

THE MD TRAINEE

"The raw material of the system"

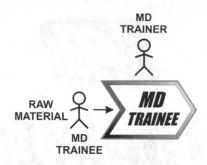

THE WRONG MATERIAL

If you run a factory, it's critical to make sure the raw materials you put in the factory are the right materials. For example, if you run a cake factory, you must have the right ingredients. And not only must the ingredients be the right ones, they must also be in the right amount. Otherwise, the outcome will be a bad cake or no cake at all.

How many times have you brought people into the system, and it turns out they do nothing or they hardly even start? One, two, five, ten, a hundred? Why do some do, while most don't? Why do some cooperate and follow the system, yet others fail to submit to the system and do simple things?

WHO'S AT FAULT?

When things go wrong, are the raw materials to blame or the factory manager who failed to bring in the right materials? When people come in with the wrong attitude, is that because of them or because of the attitude of the person bringing them in? To a large extent we're the ones to blame.

Who Wants It?

Does the new person want this business more, or do you want him to be in the business more? Does the student want to learn more, or does the teacher want to teach more?

If the new person doesn't want it more than you, he won't do it by his own will. He won't be proactive. He will be reactive. He will need to be motivated constantly.

Who's In Control?

When the trainer seems to have all the time in the world for the trainnee and the trainee doesn't have time or doesn't make time, what kind of training can you provide?

Who Follows Whom?

Should the teacher follow the student, the coach follow the player, the trainer follow the trainee? Or the other way around?

Look for the Right Material

1. If they submit license right away

What's the point of training a person when they don't even submit the paperwork to get licensed? No license, no business.

2. Meet the spouse / family

If their spouse / partner or family is not in or even against the business, how much chance is there for them to survive long-term?

3. Strong vision, great prospect list

Unless the couple sees the business, commits to develop a great PPL and continues the commitment to build more names to dominate the market, they won't have much of a future.

4. Will they go out in the field?

Not only the trainee. If the spouse supports them in the business, they can both go out in the field as well as invite people for home BPMs. This shows commitment and belief in the business. It's also critical that they learn and duplicate the business.

5. Will they buy into the mission?

It's so important that they see the financial concepts, the PFS, how we help people. They must sell out to what we do.

RECRUIT THE PERSON WHO WANTS TO JOIN.

SELL TO THE PERSON WHO WANTS TO BUY.

BUILD WITH THE PERSON WHO WANTS TO BE BUILT.

"Something to believe in.
Do they believe? Do you believe?"

THE PROSPECT LIST (PPL)

"The prospect list is where it all begins."

What's a PPL?

A PPL is a list of people who may or may not join you.

Someone you think may join may not, and someone you think may not join may.

Set No Limits for Your PPL

* Shoot for at least 100 names. Use the executive memory jogger. Everybody knows at least 200 to 300 people. Many people have more than that in their cell phone.

* Remind them this is just the beginning.

* Doing PPL is part of the job, a daily business routine.

* Highlight the top 25 prospects.

* Identify the first 5 people you will contact.

Everybody Is a Prospect

* Every person you know is a prospect.

* Every person a prospect knows is a prospect.

* Every person you have ever met and will ever meet is a prospect.

* Every person who walks, talks, and breathes within 10 feet of you is a prospect.

PROSPECT LIST MENTALITY

"You are one prospect list away from an explosion."

Most great builders are great recruiters, and, of course, great recruiters are great prospectors.

You can never do the prospect list one time and be done with your business. You must eat, sleep, and breathe PPL until you become financially independent.

> **REMEMBER:** There will be times when you try to remember somebody and you can't think of their name right away. Yet a few days later, this name will pop up.

Create a habit of prospecting. Your mind will work in miraculous ways to seek names for you.

It's so critical that you have a PPL mentality, that you duplicate it consistently with your teammates, and that they duplicate it to their teammates. Otherwise your team won't survive.

"You can never build a big team unless every one of your team members has a prospect list mentality."

THE PROSPECT LIST IS YOUR INVENTORY

Have you ever gone to a restaurant with little food in the kitchen or to a grocery store with empty shelves? How about a repair shop with no parts?

If you own a restaurant or a grocery store, your inventory is food. If you run a repair shop, your inventory are parts.

WE ARE IN THE PEOPLE BUSINESS

Our inventory is the prospect list, our lists of names. No new lists, no new names, no new inventory, and you're out of business.

- A typical person should always have a minimum of 50 names on a list at any given time to maintain activities.

- A typical baseshop should have 500+ names at any given time to have daily activities.

> If your team is struggling, the first thing you need to do is to check their prospect lists and then their agendas for appointments. You will find the answer to the problems very quickly.

"The last time many people did the prospect list was a long, long time ago."

You cannot expect to go into this business and do PPL one time only. You cannot expect to be successful by just listing a handful of your friends and relatives. You must work relentlessly to come up with more names.

PROSPECTING EVERYDAY

The key element of prospecting is regular contact with your prospects.

- Contact your prospects everyday.
- Follow up on your prospects everyday.
- Update your list everyday.

> *"You never know which name on that list will become your next superstar."*

HAVE A PROSPECT LIST WITH YOU AT ALL TIMES

> *"Don't go prospect. Prospect as you go."*

- Great prospectors are always ready to write down names. They carry a small notepad, a prospect list, or a prospect book at all times.

- A name and a phone number should be written down ASAP. Your memory rarely gives you a second chance.

- A notepad or a piece of paper will do the job. But the prospect book will keep and organize these names for the long term. It's your greatest asset. Store it. Keep it. Update it. Follow up.

> *"Maintaining a prospect list / a prospect book is like a businessperson looking into their balance sheet everyday."*

YOU GET PAID TO PROSPECT

Hypothetically speaking, if you are fully licensed, assuming you prospect 10 people and get 1 recruit, and assuming 1 recruit will generate 1 sale that is worth $1000, then each prospect is worth $100, whether they join or not.

Thus, when you contact 1 person, if they say No, don't think as if you failed. Instead, think as if you gained $100. When you contact the 2nd person, think as if you gained $200. And when you contact the 10th person, think as if you will get 1 recruit and 1 sale. Mentally, this concept can help you prospect and contact people.

> *"Salespeople look for a sale to get paid.*
> *Builders look for prospects to recruit.*
> *When recruits come, the sales will follow."*

YOUR PROSPECTS ARE YOUR NATURAL MARKET

In this industry, there are a lot of sales organizations buying leads or lists of names. They have to pay a good amount of money for these cold lists in hopes of making a sale. On the other hand, most names on our prospect list are from our warm market.

CREATE A FORTUNE LIST

Every time you add a name to your prospect list, you add to your fortune as well as their fortune. Who is so fortunate to be on your list?

> *"A prospect list can literally*
> *change your life."*

Everyday in America and the world over, there are thousands of people contacting and calling people. They don't worry about the Nos. They just pay attention to the Yeses. That is how they get paid.

3 WAYS TO DO PPL WITH A NEW RECRUIT

1. HAND OUT A TOP 25 LIST

If you hand out a Top 25 list to your new recruit and ask him to bring it back, he may never return. This person will think of endless reasons why his uncle, his sister, his cousin, his best friend, and his co-worker would not join.

If the person does come back, the list he hands you is little more than a bunch of odd names and cold numbers. You might as well open the phone book and start dialing.

2. PPL IN THE OFFICE WITHOUT THE SPOUSE

If you do the PPL in the office without the spouse, you will get a limited list. Do this only if you don't have any other option or if you need to go out in the field right away.

3. PPL IN THE HOME WITH THE SPOUSE

Doing the PPL in the home with the spouse is by far the best way to do the prospect list. When you do the prospect list in the person's home:

◆ **They open the door for you to do business with them.** The minute a team member lets me into his home, sits me down at the kitchen table, and offers me a beverage, I know we're in business.

"What's the point of recruiting a person who would not trust you?"

A SIMPLE RULE:

**If I can invite this person into
my home, and if he can invite me into his home,
we could be in business together.**

◆ **You get a chance to build a relationship with your new business partners.**

"How can you retain people if you don't know them?"

◆ **Take the time to get to know your team.** Take a slow approach and go faster rather than take a fast approach and go nowhere. I'd rather have time for 5 or 10 people than have no time for 100 people.

◆ **Take the time to quantify your team's PPL.** With your help, you can get more names from them than if they do the PPL without you.

> *"Why spend days to make a sale and not even
> have one hour to get a prospect list?
> Why recruit a person and forget the PPL
> that can bring 10 more?"*

◆ **Take the time to qualify your team's PPL.** Knowing everybody well on the list gives you priority on whom you'll have a better chance to do business with. Know their age, their job, their situation, etc. The more you know, the deeper connection you'll make.

> *"Increase effectiveness, minimize failures."*

◆ **You recruit the spouse**

One of the biggest problems we have in this business is the spouse who doesn't know what their partner is doing all night. Defuse a bomb before it explodes.

Get to know the spouse. Show her what we do. Sell her the dream. This builds great confidence for the family. You never know. She may be more excited than her husband.

◆ **You double your market**

When you do the prospect list with the husband and the wife, you enlarge your market twofold. You will get a larger prospect list and a lot more referrals.

◆ **You create a shared market**

Their prospect list is also your prospect list. Since they are on your team, it's your market too. Even if they stop doing the business, those people on the list may need your help. Thus, take time to know the names on each list.

◆ **You fast start the couple into the business**

As soon as you identify your top prospects, have the couple call the ones who live nearby.

Take the couple out in the field immediately. Show them how we do the BMP, how we Bring the Meeting to the People, and how we help families—and you've just sold them the dream all over again, and locked them into the business.

FIELD TRAIN PROSPECTING WITH YOUR TEAM

Don't just go out with your people for field training sales and recruits only. Builders love to take their people out to prospect, contact, drop by, stop by, and especially to do the prospect list.

WHICH IS MORE IMPORTANT:

- ◆ **Make 1 sale?**
- ◆ **Recruit 1 person?**
- ◆ **Get 100 names?**

When doing the prospect list at a new recruit's home, take a team member with you. That way, you help both the new recruit and you also train your team member.

"You don't need to teach them how to recruit and build. Just do it. Your actions are worth a thousand words."

DROP BY, STOP BY

"Contact many people many times."

One of the great secrets in our business is seeing people face to face. You can contact people through e-mail, snail mail, or telephone. But the most successful way to contact people is by meeting with them personally.

1. DROP BY A NEW PROSPECT

Once you quantify and qualify the PPL, you can take the new recruit to drop by their top 5 prospects, their friends, relatives, or neighbors.

Dropping by a new prospect with the new recruit is the easiest way to contact and share the opportunity.

2. DOORS OPEN

Contrary to what most people fear, most prospects are very friendly and receptive. In the last 19 years of my career, I hardly had any bad situations. The worst thing that may happen is a prospect who says they're busy or it's not the right time. In most cases, though, we're invited in with open arms, because the prospects are the friends, relatives, or neighbors of the new recruit.

> Personally, I do not like to call my brother to ask for "an appointment". I normally just ask, "Brother, are you home now? Great! I will just stop by for a short time. I have something great to show you!" Of course, if my brother is busy with something, he would tell me.

I love to drop by. I get to meet new people. I have a chance to meet both spouses. I get to see their home. I learn a lot about a couple by dropping by their home. I would never be able to do all this had I contacted the prospect on the phone.

3. ELEMENT OF SURPRISE

When I make phone contact, either I talk to the husband or the wife. Sometimes I talk to the wrong person. But when I drop by, quite often I am in for a surprise. When I think that the husband would be the one who is interested, I actually find out it's the wife. And vice versa, when I think that the wife would be the one who is interested, I actually find out it's the husband.

Other times, neither the husband nor the wife are interested, but rather the brother-in-law, the cousin, or the aunt whom I meet at the house.

4. KEEP IT SHORT

- **Don't stay too long.**

Let them know up front that you're there for a short period of time, for example, less than a half hour.

- **Give a quick overview of our business**

They key is to sell them the potential and invite them to our next BPM. If they're interested in our financial solutions, we'll schedule a PFS appointment. We do not focus on recruiting or selling at the drop by.

- **The odds for you to find a potential recruit are a lot higher**

With a drop by, you can see 3 to 5 families a night.

5. EASIER TO HANDLE OBJECTIONS

Seeing people face to face allows you to handle objections much easier than on the phone. They can see the conviction in your body language and the belief in your eyes. Also, they can't hang up on you.

Using the business review card will handle most of these situations, and if there are any questions left, tell them our manager will be the one to answer them.

6. EASIER TO UPSTART

A drop-by prospect, after joining, is much easier to upstart because we know them. We visited them at their home and became familiar with their family. They trust us more.

7. DUPLICATION

Your new recruit will duplicate what you do. They'll love to drop by and bring their team out to do BMPs. They become "field friendly" from the outset. They love to be out in the field.

8. DROP BY A TEAM MEMBER'S HOME

Drop by to see not only new prospects but also existing team members as well.

■ **Visiting a current team member builds relationship.**

Know his family. Defuse some problems that may arise with the spouse. Impart a sense of urgency to the team. They will know that you are always out in the field and that you care for them.

- **Drop by a former team member.**

Most people slow down or quit due to bad timing or temporary personal problems. Your visit can revive them. They may also give you referrals.

- **Drop by a leader.**

You should always have time for your leader. Your leader should always have time for you. This is the person that will do or die with you in the long term. Drop by, appreciate him, and appreciate his family.

9. DROP BY A CLIENT

Most clients know you well. You have been to their home 2 or 3 times already. Just say you're in the neighborhood, that you wanted to drop by to say hello. Ninety percent of the time, they will be happy to see you and appreciate your visit.

Maintain a good relationship with your clients. They're one of your best sources of referrals for more prospects, more sales, and more recruits.

"Drop by: A system whereby BMP never stops."

GETTING REFERRALS

Many people may not join or be interested in the business. But they can give referrals.

■ **Your Clients:** Your clients are a good source of referrals, but not the only one.

■ **Your Natural Market:** A lot of your family, friends, relatives, co-workers initially will not join or buy from you. But if you stay in the business, in time the referrals will come.

It's important that you always remain positive about your business and your products because they're watching you. No referrals will be given unless they see that you're happy with what you do.

In fact, some of your natural circle who did not support you when you started may change and eventually want to help you.

■ **Your Acquaintances**: You need to project an image of a successful businessperson, looking to find more people to work with you and for you. A

WHO DO YOU KNOW?

◆ **Who do you know wants to make extra income?**

◆ **Who do you know wants to have a second career?**

◆ **Who do you know is dissatisfied with their job?**

◆ **Who do you know is not happy with their business?**

friend of your brother, the person who fixes your car, the cousin of your in-laws, a person you met at a wedding or a party, etc., may be interested or refer you to someone who might be.

How to Get Referrals?

Just Ask for It

I always ask my clients, my family members, and my acquaintances to give names of people who would want to be in our business.

I ask a lot of these "Who do you know… ?" questions, and the results have been very rewarding.

"Ask many people many times."

When to Follow Up on Referrals

As Soon As Possible

A referred lead is red hot. If you don't follow up right away, you may put it off and forget about it.

After you've followed up on a client's referrals, report back to your referrer. They really appreciate you for doing that, and if you were not successful, he or she may give you another lead that is better.

"DO IT RIGHT"

MD TRAINEE

"DO IT WITH PRIDE"

SUBMIT U-4 (CANADA-LLQP)

"People Gathering"

QUALIFY FOR UPSTART
SCHOOL IN THE FIRST 10 DAYS

GO OUT <u>IN THE FIELD</u> TO:

1 DEVELOP A PROSPECT LIST

2 *<u>MATCH-UP FOR FIELD</u>*
<u>RECRUITING (BMP+BPM)</u>

3 FINALIZE YOUR PERSONAL
FINANCIAL STRATEGY

BPM + BMP

"Bring people in. Send them out.
Keep them moving."

BPM: Bring People to the Meeting
BMP: Bring the Meeting to the People

We bring the meeting to the people, then we bring people to the meeting, so that we can bring the meeting to more people, and on and on...

BPM is like an airline hub. BMP is like the flight. What's the hub without the flights? What are all the flights without the hub?

BPM + BMP must work together. We cannot run a system of BMP without BPM. And of course, BPM without BMP is very ineffective.

The more BPMs and BMPs you do, the more prospects, recruits, trainers, and builders you'll have.

It's a system whereby prospecting and recruiting never stops.

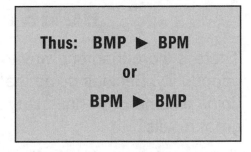

Thus: BMP ▶ BMP
or
BPM ▶ BMP

When many operations started, they had lots of BMPs and home meetings. But when they got an office, they settled down and relied on BPMs only.

BMPs should generate guests for the BPM. And recruits from the BPMs will create activities for BMPs.

BPM TOGETHER WITH BMP

Ideally, you should BMP people first, and then bring them to the BPM. They are well prepared and informed before coming into the office. A person who sees the BMP and decides to go to the BPM will probably want to join.

On the other hand, many guests are often invited directly to the BPM. They tend to be reserved and conservative because they don't know what's going on.

That's why you need the second meeting, which is the business interview at the office. But if you cannot arrange that, then instead you could follow up the BPM with a BMP at their home. You can do the presentation, the business interview, and the sign up all at the same time.

This approach is very effective, and you could meet the spouse, which can make the decision to join more solidified.

HOME BPM

There is more than one way to share the business opportunity. Besides doing the BPM at the office, doing a home BPM has many advantages and brings great results.

1. Bring It Close to Home: Sometimes, people live too far from the office. In such cases, it's much easier for guests to see the BPM at a location near their home.

2. Time Convenience: The BPM at the office happens only on certain days and certain times. Home BPMs can be done any day and any time.

3. Easier to Invite: The new recruit can invite friends, relatives, and neighbors to their home much easier than to the office.

4. Easier to Have Both the Husband and the Wife: It's easier to show the presentation to the couple at home than at the office.

5. The Recruit Becomes More Active: The new recruit takes charge of the business because it is done in his home. He tends to be passive and less involved when he goes to the office.

6. Easier to Train and Duplicate More People: When doing home BPMs, bring team members to help. They'll learn faster by doing it.

7. Best Way to Expand / Build Long Distance: Most long distance building starts with home BPMs.

"A team that has more home BMPs has more recruits, more duplication, and more leaders."

MORE AND MORE PEOPLE GO OUT IN THE FIELD,

MORE AND MORE PEOPLE GO TO THE BIG EVENT

Can you monitor these two numbers?

A lot of people pay a hundred dollars and think they're in the business. You're not in the business until you're out in the field every night.

For you to build the business, you have to ask, "Besides you, who else goes out in the field?"

When you call someone and their spouse says they're out in the field, that's where you got it made, when your down-line goes out in the field without you having to remind them.

But going out in the field in the local area is just the first test of discipline of an entrepreneur. The real test is getting people to the big event because this is the test that most people fail. Most people want to make money, but they don't want to go to the meeting.

Many people can go to big events in the local area, but once you put it a little far away, then you find out the real truth. The problem is when you have the event close by, they show up late, and when they show up, they don't listen. But if you put the event far away, usually they show up early and they do study. It's funny. I don't know how to explain that, but that's the way it is.

You can only build people through this thing. You build people by having them go out in the field every night, and you build people by having them go to the big event, because through the big event they are built.

I don't want to build people. I don't want to train people. People, you cannot tell them to do anything. But at the big event, they listen, and they listen to somebody else.

All you have to do is find the right kind of people. But you can never find the right kind of people. You just got to find a lot of people and let them go out in the field and see if they go to the big event, and the system will help them or eliminate them.

CR

THE SIMPLE PRESENTATION

"The Secret of the BMP"

The whole purpose of the BMP is to make it duplicat-able. People must be able to copy you in a short period of time. They must say to themselves, "It's so simple, I can do it!"

1. Short

We don't want to have to be there all night. The presentation should be less than a half hour. What good is it if you spend 3 hours to recruit a person only to have your trainee depressed by the difficulty of recruiting and the amount of information you have to have to do the job?

2. Simple

We want the new person to be able to memorize the presentation and duplicate us fast. Most people should be able to begin reciting your presentation after the third viewing.

3. Don't Answer Questions

The purpose of the BMP is to share the good news about our financial concepts and our business. We don't plan to recruit or to make a sale. If they like the business, we invite them to our BPM. If they like the financial solutions, we schedule them to see one of our licensed experts to do the PFS.

A "SICKENINGLY SIMPLE" PRESENTATION

Personally after watching the simple
presentation 3 or 4 times, I feel very itchy to
present it myself. By the time I've watched
8 of them, I was able to remember just about
every line, every transition, every word.
Listening to the simple presentation
over and over made me sick.
I almost couldn't stand it anymore and couldn't
wait to go out and do it myself.

Thus, if they have any questions, we refer them to see our manager.

4. SPEED

Since it's short and simple, we can see many people in one night.

5. DUPLICATABLE

Trainees should be able to do the presentation in 7 days by themselves. Since it is short and simple, and since they don't have to handle questions or objections, trainees have no fear to go out in the field on their own.

*"After 7 days, are your people ready to go out
and do presentations, or are they still calling you
to take them out?"*

Psychology of the Presentation
BMP/BPM

"Fundamentally, the marksman aims at himself."

— ZEN IN THE ART OF ARCHERY

It's not about the details. It's the reason behind. When you do the presentation, you don't just sell the business, you sell your belief.

When you go through concepts such as the X Curve and the Rule of 72, you are not only talking about financial solutions but really

> **THE TRUE POINTS OF YOUR PRESENTATION ARE:**
>
> • Selling the belief in the Mission
> • Selling the belief in the Vision

ly how much they make a positive difference for families, and especially your own family.

And when you talk about a vision of a new industry, you are literally selling them your vision, your belief in how you see yourself and this company becoming very successful in the future.

MY FIRST 8 BMPs

I saw the opportunity in May 1985 at a Saturday morning BPM. I made an appointment for noon the next Monday. I was so excited I joined right away, bought the product Tuesday, and went out in the field that same night to do BMPs. I started right. I scheduled 3 appointments for the first night because the trainer insisted on a minimum of 3 appointments to go out with me.

The first appointment was at my brother-in-law's home. He is so close to me, so I knew he would do business with us. But he didn't. Then, I took my trainer to the home of my best friend, a sophisticated engineer. He did not show any reaction to the presentation. He was stone-faced the entire time and never even said a word, not even a No. At the third appointment, another friend showed some interest but wanted to think it over.

I was stunned, I thought all 3 of them would be very receptive, or at least one would, but not even one responded positively. I told my trainer that tomorrow will be better and kept apologizing for the first 3 failures.

The next day, I brought my trainer to 3 more places, and again, nobody showed any interest, just a few questions and remarks. I was so disappointed. We've been to 6 houses already. I had to do something the 3rd night, but I couldn't get 3 appointments. I only had 2. I called my trainer and asked her to give me another chance and apologized because I could only find 2 appointments.

Nothing came out of those 2 appointments. My first 8 BMPs were all failures. I almost wanted to quit. I was so mad. I did not understand why the closest people to me all said "No" or "I want to think about it".

But I couldn't quit. The thought of being a social worker for the rest of my life was even more painful. Also, I thought that we did good BMPs. In fact, we did everything right. After I thought about it, I realized there was no problem with our business or our presentation. It was their problem. I swallowed my pain and went on.

The first year in the business, I was bad, but I learned a lot. I learned that this business is not as easy as I thought. I learned that even brothers, best friends, and cousins will not do business with me. I learned to move on and to stay excited, even while being hurt. I learned that it was critical to go out as a team, me and the trainer, so we can motivate each other to keep going on. I did not take this thing for granted, and I prepared myself for a long fight toward my independence.

ᘓᖇ

BUILDER'S NOTE:

Although all 8 BMPs were not successful, one very positive thing came out of it. I was duplicated! I saw 8 simple presentations over and over again. I memorized it by heart. I was able to do it. There was no real secret. After that I knew I could go out in the field by myself, which I did. Also, most of the people eventually either joined or bought from me. Some did so a few months later on, others took a year. And the rest is history.

WHAT IS "SELLING THE DREAM"?

This is what we sell:

- Be Somebody

- Be My Own Boss

- Own My Own Business

- Control My Destiny

- Great Income

- Financial Security

- Provide for My Family

- Do Great Things for People

- Travel Nationwide and Worldwide

- Build Nationwide and Worldwide Business

"Don't sell them your dream. Sell them the dream that is most important to them."

YOU SHOULD HAVE BPMS REGULARLY

3 PURPOSES OF THE BPM:

1. Resell the dream to existing team members

2. Teach current teammates how to sell the dream

3. Sell the dream to new prospects

We need to do the BPM many times a week (at least every 3 to 4 days) because:

- When people are prospecting, inviting, doing the BMP, and recruiting, they need to bring these new guests or team members to the office as soon as possible.

- Just like a car, which needs to be refueled regularly, our teammates need to be recharged, energized, and motivated after being beat up in the field.

- Our trainers and trainees need to be recognized for their efforts and to share their success stories. They can also share their experiences of what it's like to be a crusader and how they make a difference for families.

- Regular BPMs are predictable and convenient for leaders, teammates, upline, and downline to meet with each other to train, plan, and share crucial information.

■ If you do BPMs only once a week, the cycle of business slows down tremendously. It will be harder to find and build serious and committed people.

"What would you do if your car ran out of gas and you had to wait the whole week before you could get it refueled?"

BUILDER'S TRAP:
Don't ever miss a meeting. Don't ever miss the BPM. Don't even show any sign of tiredness or lack of enthusiasm in the BPM. Your team will recognize it and won't show up.

DAYTIME BPM

For so long we did meetings during the evenings and weekends, assuming that most people have to go to work. We forgot that there are a lot of people who would prefer to do our business on weekdays during regular working hours. So by doing the BPM in the day time, we attract a bigger, diversified market.

STAY AT HOME SPOUSES

Most housespouses have time from morning until about 3pm, when their children come home from school. In Japan, one of the largest securities companies built the majority of their sales force based largely on housewives.

LADIES

Many women feel safer going to meetings and doing the business during the daytime rather than at night.

PEOPLE WORKING AT DIFFERENT SHIFTS

Nurses, students, teachers, food service workers, factory workers, etc. may be busy working at night.

PROFESSIONALS / SELF EMPLOYED

CPAs, lawyers, doctors, real estate agents and others have flexible schedules and may prefer daytime business meetings.

UNEMPLOYED / BETWEEN JOBS

These people are free during the day.

REGULAR EMPLOYED PEOPLE

If it's important enough, people can ask for 1 to 2 hours off from work to come see the business.

AND MORE...

"The more BPMs, the more potential recruits, the bigger the market you penetrate."

MOZONE: THE ENVIRONMENT TO RECRUIT AND BUILD

*"MoZone: The Momentum Zone.
It's an environment of energy,
positivity, excitement, and power!"*

It's the atmosphere, the ambience that counts. In any entertainment center where there are many people—a restaurant, a shopping mall, a show business—the environment is critical.

When people feel good, they do good. When people feel intimidated or reserved, they tend to close their minds.

Always maintain a good environment in the office, especially during the BPM. The BPM is show time for our business. It's our opening days. It's show off day for one of the best businesses and careers in the world!

> **BUILDER'S TRAP:** A good environment doesn't have to be artificially "plastic fantastic". It must be natural and sincere. So don't overdo it. The new guests or new team members may feel intimidated. It may seem to them that we're begging and bugging.

*"It pays to smile, to be excited, and to be positive.
What a business!"*

THE *10* COMMANDMENTS OF MOZONE

1. **SIT IN FRONT**

2. **EYE CONTACT**

3. **WALK FASTER**

4. **TALK LOUDER**

5. **SMILE**

6. **DRESS SHARP**

7. **COME EARLY, STAY LATE**

8. **DECLARE YOUR INTENTIONS PUBLICLY**

9. **RAISE UP, STAND UP**

10. **STUMBLE FORWARD, STAY CONFUSED**

"It's what's inside of you that counts."

10 WAYS TO BUILD YOUR CONFIDENCE

1. SIT IN FRONT

When I was a kid, I sat in the front row of the class. As I got to high school, I eventually moved to the middle. And by the time I went to college, I found myself in the back of the class.

Ever since, I always took a back seat in my life. I always sat behind, hid behind someone else, lost myself in the crowd. In most situations, I was content and sometimes happy about it. Nobody bothered me. Nobody looked at me or said anything to me. But with a price, I realized that I was not winning.

> *"In a dogsled, if you're not the lead dog,*
> *the scenery doesn't change much."*

Being a short guy, sitting in the back, I gave up a lot. I didn't see most things ahead, except for other people's hair. I was passive, non-engaged, and frustrated. I was behind. And I found most people were like me.

In our BPM, for instance, if we set 10 rows of chairs, most people will come in and start sitting down at the 10th row first. If we set 3 rows, they will sit in the 3rd row. Very few people come in and sit in front. Even team members prefer to sit in the back.

One day, when reading The Magic of Thinking Big by Dr. David J. Schwartz, who suggested some simple techniques to build confidence, it hit me like a ton of bricks. I realized what went wrong! I made an effort to change. "I will sit in front from now on," I told myself.

What a big change! It looked easy, but it's not that easy to do. Being a front-seater will change your life. You will be fully engaged. You will be a student of the business. You will be coachable.

When you sit in the front, you take charge. You're at the front line. You listen more attentively. You have no distractions. You're totally focused. Your business mindset rises to a new level.

> *"Great leaders always sit in front,*
> *fight for the front, and are always ready."*

Sitting in front will lead your life down the winner's track. Not sitting in front could cost you and your team tons of money.

2. EYE CONTACT

I was a shy kid who was afraid to talk to people, let alone look in their eyes. People told me it's not polite to look into older people's eyes. The fear of people grew inside me. I could sit next to another person at a party for hours without saying a word, as if I was playing a silence endurance contest. Not surprisingly, I didn't feel too good about myself.

This business was so uncomfortable for me at first. had to contact people. I had to say something and look at people. But over the years, that was one of the best things that could have happened to me.

I learned to look straight in people's eyes. I could see through them. I could communicate with them. More often, eye contact speaks louder than words.

"Making eye contact establishes trust,
confidence, and positivity
with the person you communicate with."

Now, I feel a lot more effective meeting people face to face rather than talking with them on the phone. I'm confident and more comfortable with people as a result.

3. WALK FASTER

Your actions and your feeling go together. When you're sad, you walk slow. When you're happy, you walk faster. When you walk faster, you tend to be happier.

The environment you're in will also affect your actions and your feeling. When you listen to upbeat music, you are active and you move quicker. A sad song will slow you down. Even my car can recognize that. When I am sad, my car drives slower. But when I'm excited, my car gains speed.

Most of us wait until we feel good before we do something. Running a business based on our feelings is dangerous. The renown basketball star Jerry West said, "You can't get much done in life if you only work on the days when you feel good."

We can control our feeling. We can control our actions. We can control our life. Just walk faster. You'll find yourself a happier, more positive person.

"Hurry up! Get the job done.
There are a lot of things in life
waiting for you to do, to see, and to enjoy."

4. TALK LOUDER

When you're sad or tired, you talk in a low voice. When you are energetic and happy, you speak louder.

So it doesn't matter much what you say. What matters are the tone of your voice, the expression on your face, and the movement of your body.

> **IT'S SAID THAT THE IMPACT OF COMMUNICATION COMES:**
> 55% from body language
> 38% from the tone of your voice
> 7% from verbal content

Just raise your voice one notch, you will feel stronger.

"Every time I call home, my wife can tell right away if I had a good day or a bad one."

5. SMILE

"The world's best way to communicate."

A smile affects people more than anything else. A smile builds quick confidence and changes the environment around you.

One day at the doctor's office, most people seemed to be quiet, sad, or worried—until a lady came in with her child. The minute the kid smiled, the atmosphere in the waiting room lit up. Everyone smiled, became happy, and began to talk to each other. Amazing what a smile can do.

"When you smile, you change your attitude, and you change the attitude of the people around you.

6. DRESS SHARP

I used to dress down, very casually, and proud of it. It seemed as if I wanted the whole world to know that I'm a social worker, I'm poor, I'm care free, I'm taking it easy.

I got what I wanted. Nobody paid attention to me. Nobody took me seriously. Nobody talked any business with me. One of my cousins joined a company for months and never bothered to recruit me. One day, after I joined another person, I met him at a meeting. His first words were: "I never thought that you would want to be in business?!"

Having a habit of dressing properly and looking sharp changed my outlook on life.

"If you dress up, you move up.
If you dress down, you move down."

When you dress sharp, you feel better and look more professional. People don't want to follow a sloppy-looking leader. Your appearance is very important. You don't have to be too formal or flashy, so long as you do not intimidate our guest, our client, or our potential business partner. You should also ask your guest to dress properly. The BPM is a business meeting. But don't be too strict, especially with your first-time guest.

7. COME EARLY - STAY LATE

Most people come to the office on time or a little late, as if they go to work. On a BPM night, they come in, unprepared, lost in the crowd, hoping that their guest is somewhere in the MoZone area, hoping that their upline won't be disappointed, hoping that their down-line won't get mad at them. I know. I was one of them.

The day I happened to come to the meeting an hour early, I saw a totally different picture. I saw a lot of work to prepare for. The chairs, the microphone, the parking lot, the speakers, the trainers, the name tags, the sign-in sheets, the kits. I saw a business at work!

The minute the BPM ends, most people head to the parking lot and go home. I was one of them. Just like in any job, can't wait to get out. Just like in any class-room, can't wait for the bell to ring.

"I'm tired, I'm hungry, and I want to go home."

However, when I got home, most of the time I did nothing special like watching TV or reading maga-zines for hours.

Then, one day, I decided to stay late. I saw a totally different picture. The meeting after the meeting. Setting goals. Getting commitments. Leaders staying after the meeting to help serious people create a business plan, monitor activities, and do paperwork.

After the meeting, people open up, the serious builders stay late, and the team goes to get a late snack. It's their time to build relationships. They talk about the business in an informal way. They share a lot of insight and observation on how to improve each other's business.

"When you come early and stay late, you're in control. You're in the business."

Successful businesspeople show up to work early. Successful system builders master this challenge. Since you go the meeting anyway, why don't you come early, stay late, and spend an extra hour? This extra hour gives you an entrepreneur mentality that most employees will hardly ever know!

8. DECLARE YOUR INTENTIONS PUBLICLY

You can't change or hit your goal unless you declare it and let many people know. It's easier to quit smoking if you let everyone around you know your intention. If you have a goal, declare it. The goal is half done.

9. RAISE UP, STAND UP

> *"Stand for something you believe in.*
> *Raise up to your dream."*

When it comes to some challenge or task, many people can hardly stand up or raise up. For many of us, the last time we raised our hand or stood up was in high school.

Even if people raise up, they can hardly raise their hand high, pass their head. And even if they stand up, they can hardly stand up long enough.

It seems like people go through life carrying too much baggage. They were put down too many times. They got shafted by their boss, pulled down by their co-worker, or criticized by their family. Their shoulders get heavy, their body worn out. Raising up is hard to do.

10. STUMBLE FORWARD, STAY CONFUSED

Moving forward may seem risky, but doing nothing is even riskier.

You can't wait until you know everything before you do something. You can't wait until all conditions are right before you start something.

"Success is never convenient."

Before success, you must fail first. Those who never try never learn.

Your activities create knowledge, but your knowledge won't create activities.

I often hear: "Show me everything. When I get all my licenses, I'll do it, big!" Unfortunately, that rarely happens! Usually these people don't even last long enough to get licensed.

Many employees stumble forward easily when their boss gives them orders. But when they come to us, they become shaky and hesitant.

"Action fights fear.
Inaction creates more fear.
Walk right through your fear,
and the death of fear is certain."

MISTAKES TO AVOID AT THE BPM

SHOWING UP ON TIME

If you show up on time, you're too late. You and your guest will have missed the whole point of the BPM: the Magic of MoZone. As a rule of thumb, teammates should be at the office at least a half hour before the meeting, and leaders should be at the office at least an hour before the meeting.

> **IF YOU ARE ON TIME, YOU'RE TOO LATE.**

BRINGING A BAD DAY TO THE BPM

When you walk into the office, please leave your troubles behind. I know that life is tough out there, but we are in the people business. People at the office don't need to know about personal problems, a traffic jam, bad weather, or a car accident.

Our business is selling happiness, a "can do" spirit, a chance to make dreams come true. So when you enter the office, show that you're happy about what you do. Show that you're determined to win.

WAITING FOR GUESTS IN THE PARKING LOT

Do not show that you are so desperate. If guests can find the parking lot, they can find their way into the office.

EITHER YOU'RE IN OR YOU'RE OUT, BUT DON'T HANG AROUND

When you're at a meeting, stay in the meeting. The BPM hours are your working hours. It's your job to learn from other trainers, to work the system, and to build your business. It is not a time to hide in the office and use the computer or go outside and talk on the phone. Your team may duplicate that. Other teams may duplicate it. You not only hurt your business. You end up hurting other people's business as well.

Acting Casual to a First-Time Guest

Every time one of your guests walks out of the BPM room, you have to be excited, even if you've listened to the BPM thousands of times already. You cannot act casual. You have to treat every guest like your first. Don't ever forget where you come from. Do you remember the first time you saw the presentation? Wasn't that powerful?

Recommending What They Should Do

When the BPM is over, and you meet with your guests, what you say to them is so crucial. Instead of asking them what they think, can you say something positive and affirmative? Can you say, "Is that awesome? Was that a great presentation? This is an incredible opportunity, right? The presenter is powerful, right?" This is what you recommended them to see in the first place.

Doing the Business Interview Before the Business Interview

Sometimes your guest is excited and curious to know more about the business and begins to ask questions. And you, also excited, begin to answer their questions. You do your upline's job too early. You do the business interview before the business interview.

Remember:
Don't talk too much. Especially when you're not ready, when you don't know how to answer, or when you're not in control of the situation.

Instead of answering their questions, can you say, "Wonderful. Those are great questions. I'm glad you're interested. Write them down. I'm sure when you come back tomorrow to see my Marketing Director, she will answer all your questions."?

"The presentation in the BPM is to recruit.

The presentation in the parking lot is to destroy."

USING THE BUSINESS REVIEW CARD

Using the business review card is more convenient and less confusing. We show the presentation, share the information, and they make the decision.

It's also very duplicatable. Everyone can do it. Just give them the card. Either they want to take a look at the business, or they want to understand more about our financial concepts and solutions. They will tell us what they want.

MONKEY BUSINESS

"Monkey see, monkey do." In the duplication business, your people duplicate what you do good or bad. And your people always do more than you. When you come 5 minutes late, your people come 10 minutes late. When you don't show up for 1 meeting, your people don't show up for 3 meetings. If you don't show up for one month, your people don't show up forever.

MAKING THE BUSINESS INTERVIEW APPOINTMENT

Work with Your MD/Trainer to Set Up an Appointment

Understand that your MD/trainer is not making an appointment for herself but rather for you. Do yourself a favor. Don't side with your guest and say he's too busy to make an appointment. Your MD understands that your guest has a job and a family. But you need to encourage him in any way you can to meet with your upline within 24 to 48 hours during the daytime. We need to talk to the guest while they're still excited.

Hold the Business Interview within 24 to 48 Hours

If you don't set up an appointment within 24 to 48 hours, the odds for the prospect to come back for the business interview are very low. When a typical guest goes home, he will talk to his spouse, his cousin, and his friends. These people are going to rain on his parade with all sorts of negative comments: "You can't sell... There's no way you can do this..." That's why the sooner we see them, the better chance we have of answering their questions and saving them.

Do the Business Interview at the Office

Normally, when you do the business interview in the office, you have more control. But if you have guests at the BPM who don't show up for the business interview, they probably got shot down by the doom-

and-gloom crowd. In that case, you have to follow up the BPM with a BMP and recruit them at their house.

PRECONDITION YOUR GUEST TO MAKE AN APPOINTMENT

Before you bring your guest to your MD, tell your guest that your MD is a busy person and that an appointment needs to be set tomorrow or the next day during the daytime. Say something such as, "Joe, my MD is a very busy lady. You have to see her tomorrow. Otherwise, other people will take up all her time. Usually her evenings are always booked helping her clients. So you have to find some time tomorrow during the day to see her. If you can take an hour or two off work, it will be well worth your time."

FOLLOW UP

Follow up for good measure. Call him up to remind him about the appointment. If you sense he has been negatively affected by his friends or family, offer to give him a ride to the appointment and reassure him that this is a legitimate opportunity.

"DO IT RIGHT"

MD TRAINEE

"DO IT WITH PRIDE"

SUBMIT U-4 (CANADA-LLQP)

"People Gathering"

QUALIFY FOR UPSTART SCHOOL IN THE FIRST 10 DAYS

GO OUT <u>IN THE FIELD</u> TO:

1 DEVELOP A PROSPECT LIST

2 MATCH-UP FOR FIELD RECRUITING (BMP+BPM)

3 *<u>FINALIZE YOUR PERSONAL FINANCIAL STRATEGY</u>*

PERSONAL FINANCIAL STRATEGY

After a person joins, we need to sit down with that person and their spouse to go through the financial strategy to take care of their family.

1. THEY NEED TO UNDERSTAND OUR CONCEPTS AND PRODUCTS

What we do is so critical for families. From proper needs for protection to long term investments, from managing debt to increasing cash flow, from creating an emergency fund to preserving their estate, every one of these concepts can change their lives and their family's lives for generations to come. The reason we grow is because we provide such badly needed information and services to Middle America.   I remember when I first saw the Rule of 72, I thought it was the eighth wonder of the world.

2. THEY NEED TO BE HELPED

People don't need to buy our products to work for our company. But it's critical that they know information about and solutions to their personal finances. They need to know their current situation and what they should do to take care of their family's financial security. And if they have the need and are suitable, they should own the appropriate products as soon as they can.

3. THEY NEED TO BELIEVE IN OUR MISSION

The best way to help new recruits understand what we do for the consumer out there is to see how it helps them first.

Practice what you preach. Help people understand
and believe in our six steps to financial security. It's
easier for them to be successful in a business that
they believe in and that does good things for people.

4. SHARE, DON'T SELL

A normal salesperson would sell anything the consumer wants to buy, even if that person doesn't own
the product. Crusaders share what they believe in and
recommend to others what they would do for themselves. You don't really need to sell.

WHAT'S A CRUSADER?
WHAT'S OUR MISSION?

"Do it right. Do it with pride."

We use the words crusade and mission often. What do they mean in our business?

A crusader is someone who believes in what he or she is doing. They do the right thing. It also means that when they sell a product, they make sure that their clients understand all the advantages as well as the disadvantages of the product. The clients will only buy if it is good and suitable for them and their family.

Our mission is to make a difference for families, to help build wealth for families. Our crusade is to share with people our financial concepts, so they can increase their cash flow, manage their debt, create an emergency fund, provide proper protection for the family, build long-term assets, and preserve their estate.

Likewise, when we recruit new members, we must tell them the advantages as well as the challenges of the business.

> **Our mission is to make a difference for families, to help build wealth for families.**

UNDERSTAND THE FIRST BLOCK OF THE MD FACTORY

I. THE FIRST DIMENSION

"DO IT RIGHT"

MD TRAINEE

"DO IT WITH PRIDE"

SUBMIT U-4 (CANADA-LLQP)

QUALIFY FOR UPSTART
SCHOOL IN THE FIRST 10 DAYS

GO OUT <u>IN THE FIELD</u> TO:

1. DEVELOP A PROSPECT LIST
2. MATCH-UP FOR FIELD RECRUITING (BMP+BPM)
3. FINALIZE YOUR PERSONAL FINANCIAL STRATEGY

---

7 STEP DUPLICATION

"7 & 7: Complete the 7 Steps in 7 Days."

1. Submit U-4
2. Meet the Spouse
3. Prospect List
4. Field Presentation BMP
5. Personal Financial Strategy
6. Recruit 3 Direct
7. Duplication

"The perfect copy machine."

II. THE 2ND DIMENSION

People Gathering

Why do you have to do prospect list, go out in the field to do BMP or invite people to the BPM, and do the PFS?

The purpose is to gather as many people as possible to join our business. And of course, to bring in as many potential MD trainees.

At the least, you should gather 3 people to qualify for MD Club.

III. THE 3RD DIMENSION

The Crusade

In the first block of the system, during the early stages

of the business, the new MD trainee must see the goodness of the business, what we do to help people. It should be the mission, not the commission or the money, that impresses them.

IV. THE 4TH DIMENSION

Trust

We have to establish a relationship and develop the trust factor. That's the reason why we come to the MD trainee's home to talk to the spouse. If the couple doesn't trust us, it will be hard to get things started.

V. THE 5TH DIMENSION

Duplication

Everything we do in the first block will be duplicated. Either we duplicate good or we duplicate bad. Either we do it right or we do it wrong. Whether we make it complicated or we keep it simple, the trainee will copy us. Like most things in life, the first step is so critical. We may not have a second chance.

> By the end of the 1st block, usually after the first 7 days, the new MD trainee will draw one of two conclusions:
>
> 1. "Wow, it looks good. It looks simple. It seems doable. I can do this!" With this mindset things will start out great.
>
> 2. "Gee! It's all quite confusing. I need to learn more. I'm not sure if I can do it..." If he has these thoughts, there will be a long hard road ahead and he may not make it at all.

THE 4TH DIMENSION

*"Without trust from the family, you cannot get
a person to move."*

THE TRUST FACTOR

It's a pain to work with somebody who doesn't trust you.
How in the world does somebody join you one day and
3 days later on disappear? How does somebody listen
to you one day and the next day doesn't believe a word
you say? Something happened in between.

THE HIDDEN REASON

In many cases people quit not because of the product
or market conditions, but because of their spouse.
Without support from the spouse, succeeding in this
business is a losing battle.

SOLVE THIS PROBLEM EARLY ON

The minute a new person joins, tell them, "I need to
see you and your spouse tonight at your home. Can
you please finish dinner early, so we're ready to talk
about business?"

If she asks, "What for?" you answer, "To get you
started." The minute she says yes, she trusts you
enough to let you in her home.

GAIN TRUST - PRESENT THE BUSINESS

The reason you need to go to her home is to gain trust
and show the business to the spouse. If the spouse is
busy, you should wait until they're available. Or if he
can't see you, you should reschedule. You want them
to know you're serious about this business.

When both husband and wife agree to sit down with you, then you talk to them, because you need to explain to both of them. You should not explain to only one of them and let her explain to her husband. Both don't have to do the business, but they both need to believe in what we do.

THE ONLY WAY TO BUILD IS WITH A COUPLE

The short time you spend with this family is the best investment you'll ever make with them. You'll find out right away if this is the family you're going to work with, or if there's no hope.

> Have you ever known a woman let her husband go out every night and she doesn't know what he's doing? It happened to me. The first few weeks I went out in the field, my wife received a call from a cousin telling her she saw me driving around with a good looking woman.

NO TRUST, NO WORK

The minute they trust you they give you a good prospect list. And when they trust you they don't mind taking you to see those people.

But if they don't trust you, they're not going to give you a real prospect list. Instead they hand you a list of people who, whether they join or not, don't affect them.

GET TO KNOW THE REAL FAMILY

At the home you meet the real family. At the office you are different people. But at the home you're real people.

MAKE A GOOD FIRST IMPRESSION

You come to their home, and the first impression is a good one. You show them a real business. You're committed. You care. You're serious. You're a person with a mission and a dream. You believe in what you do. You're absolutely positive. Your new recruit and her husband are fired up. The first appointment at her house determines the rest of her career, because at the first appointment she feels like rainbows.

BUILD IT RIGHT FROM DAY ONE

The new recruit joins in the morning and that evening you're at their home. The next thing you do is take her out to her friends' and relatives' homes. Do you need to explain to her that this is a home-based business?

And when you take her out, she may have some doubts, but the minute you sit down with her friends and relatives, you show the crusade, what we do for families. The information is so powerful and wonderful. You show it with all your conviction. And you treat her friends and relatives with respect and kindness. Don't you think your new recruit is proud about what we do?

Thus you have a builder because she loves to go out in the field. She falls in love with the business from day one. And when she recruits somebody, she wants to go to people's homes. The minute she gets licensed, she can't wait to go out to people's homes. She can't wait to take her downline to people's homes.

"I'd rather recruit 2 people and do it right than recruit 10 people and do it wrong. I'd rather recruit 2 people and build people who trust me than recruit 10 people who don't trust me, don't know me, and don't want to work with me seriously."

LISTEN CAREFULLY

When you listen:

The 1st time,

you may like it.

The 2nd time,

you understand it.

The 3rd time,

you feel it.

The 4th time,

you memorize it.

The 5th time,

you apply it.

BE A CONFIDENT LEADER, NOT A CONFUSED SQUANDERER

LEADING	SQUANDERING
■ BPM/BMP with conviction	◆ Doing a presentation
■ Show Vision and Mission	◆ A part-time business
■ "We're looking for serious, committed, hardworking individuals."	◆ "We will accommodate you and work with you whenever you're available."
■ "I'll see you at 7pm with your spouse at your home."	◆ "May I come to your house tonight?"
■ We are going to fill out the U-4 now, and you bring back the fingerprint card at 6pm tomorrow."	◆ "Here's the U-4. Go home and fill it out."
■ "We expect you to be licensed in 3 months and become a MD in 6 months."	◆ "Can you finish licensing in 3 months and become a MD in 6 months?"

■ "Let's work together and answer all the questions as I go through the Prospect List process."	◆ "Think of people who may join you and write their names down."
■ Definite	◆ Iffy
■ Clear, concise	◆ Confused, ambiguous
■ Confident	◆ Worried about losing the recruit
■ Tell them all the challenges of starting up the business.	◆ Keep telling them how great this business is and convincing them that it will be worth their time.
■ Show them every step they need to do and every step you are going to do with them.	◆ No schedule for them. No schedule for you with them.
■ Show them the next step.	◆ "I'll see you next week."
■ Make things happen and expect results.	◆ "Please try your best."

"The Big Push"

RECRUIT 3
QUALIFY FOR MD CLUB

BUILD:

LEVEL 1: 1 MD CLUB LEG
LEVEL 2: 2 MD CLUB LEGS
LEVEL 3: 3 MD CLUB LEGS

MD CLUB

"The Big Push"

The purpose of MD Club is to make a big push to become MD.

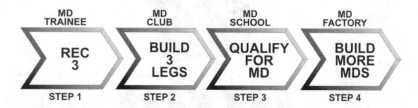

As you can see, the system is quite simple.

STEP 1

When you start, you recruit 3.

STEP 2

Then at the MD Club level, you duplicate that process with these 3 recruits to build them into 3 legs (L1, L2, L3: Leg 1, Leg 2, Leg 3).

STEP 3

You qualify for MD.

STEP 4

You build more MDs.

If you look at this MD Factory chart, the whole system depends on building MD Club members.

Thus, MD club is the building block of the system. You must qualify for MD Club and build MD Club. You must recruit 3, and help those 3 qualify for MD Club, and continue the duplication process.

RECRUIT 3 MENTALITY

Once a person finds the first 3, there will be no stopping him to recruit more. Most importantly, during the initial stages when he recruits 3, he must go through all the experiences of how to recruit these first 3 people, i.e., PPL, BMP, drop by, follow up.

DUPLICATION: L1, L2, L3

This mentality must be duplicated to build 3 legs, the foundation for a solid base.

If a person qualifies for MD Club but fails to help his team members qualify for MD Club, the system won't work.

Also, the MD must overlap leadership and jump down and help make sure everyone qualifies for MD Club.

THE MD CLUB

"The Simple System to Build MDs"

MD CLUB QUALIFICATIONS:
- Submit U-4
- Recruit 3 direct

SIMPLE PROCESS:
1. Submit U-4

2. Qualify for MD Club

3. Run for MD

SIMPLE RECOGNITION:
1. Submit U-4

2. MD Club Shirt

3. MD Jacket

WHY MD CLUB:
- Focus new associate on MD from the start.
- Recruit to build a solid organization. Implant a recruiting mentality from the get go.
- Retention. If everyone qualifies for MD Club, they'll likely be here for the long haul.
- Expect new associate to qualify for MD Club in the first 7 days.

THE MD CLUB MEETING AFTER THE MEETING

"It's easier to work with the committed."

Create a culture of focusing on MD in the baseshop and at the early stages. Identify the "want to do" versus the "one who really does it".

MONITOR:

- Checklist
- Organization chart
- Activities and results / minimum 3 points a week
- Expect activities to be scheduled and results in the next seven days
- Set up a deadline for license and MD promotion

MOTIVATE:

- Welcome new qualifiers
- Recognize their goals and their dreams
- Build relationships among club members
- Recognize achievers, big and small

TRAIN:

- Train skills and wills of the MDs to be
- Involve club members into the business: set up, parking, meeting, convention, training, compliance, etc.
- Build up their presentation skills, their leadership skills, and their confidence

COMPETE:

- Foster an environment of competition
- People tend to rise to the level of their group. "If he can do it and she can do it, then I can do it."
- Competition eliminates fear.

SYSTEMATIZE:

- Building a baseshop, building new MDs becomes a system. Young / small MDs can work with other MDs to build, reducing the fear of young MDs with small baseshops.
- More strength and faster speed are necessary to build MDs
- Club members encourage and help each other to become MD

KEEP IT SIMPLE

"Flow, not form."

FLOW	FORM
Simplify	Complicate
Unify	Divide
Multiply	Fragment

MD CLUB MEMBERS MUST KNOW HOW TO DO BMP

"A MD Club member is not a non-MD.
It's a MD in the making."

MD CLUB MEMBERS MUST BECOME MD CLUB TRAINERS

- Follow MD to the field.
- Practice and master the presentation.
- Organize and support the Home BPM.
- Do BMP. Take new recruit out to the field.
- Duplicate / build new MD Club members.

> **Once the MD Club member becomes a Trainer, she can take people out in the field and duplicate herself.**

VISION OF PROMOTION

Which one looks more simple?

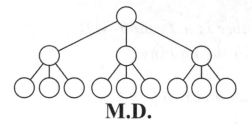

M.D.

MD Club

Each just focuses to qualify for MD club.
"Becoming an MD just got easier"

POWER OF THE MD CLUB

Build wide and deep

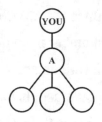

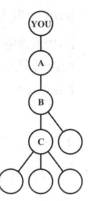

WHICH ORGANIZATION DO YOU PREFER?

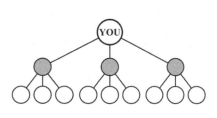

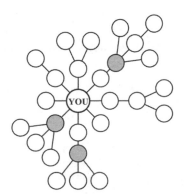

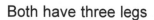

Both have three legs

FAST START

"It is critical to have a strong start."

A NEW RECRUIT NEEDS TO HAVE A FAST START WITHIN 72 HOURS

It's easier to strike while the iron is still hot. When he's excited, he's willing to start right away. But his enthusiasm can fade away quickly, especially when he begins to face some negativity or rejection.

PROCRASTINATION IS A PART OF HUMAN NATURE

Whenever possible, most people tend to wait it out and see what happens before doing anything. A common response is: "Once I know it, then I will do it." If people have a choice between challenging and easy, they always gravitate toward the easy way out. Thus, most of them opt to get licensed before they do anything. They'd rather learn by studying rather than learn by doing.

> If people have a choice between challenging and easy, they always gravitate toward the easy way out.

As a result, many fired up recruits quickly lose interest, and fear begins to set in. Licensing becomes a boring, tedious process. Most end up not getting licensed, or if they ever do, it drags on a long time. Worse, when they get licensed, they have no team and nobody to sell to. They become lonely licensed agents.

> ## FAST START THE NEW RECRUIT TO MD CLUB
>
> **A new recruit who starts fast tends to duplicate a fast start to his team. A recruit who starts slow tends to duplicate failure to his team.**

FAST START TO SPARK AN EXPLOSION

But if we can get them to go out with a trainer to recruit a few people, they'll explode with renewed enthusiasm. The chances of retention and of finishing licensing will be a lot higher. Help them qualify for MD Club, and you'll have a winner.

"It's hard to ask someone to fast start if you yourself move like a snail."

CAN YOU WALK AND CHEW GUM AT THE SAME TIME?

What would you prefer to do?

OPTION A   **OPTION B**

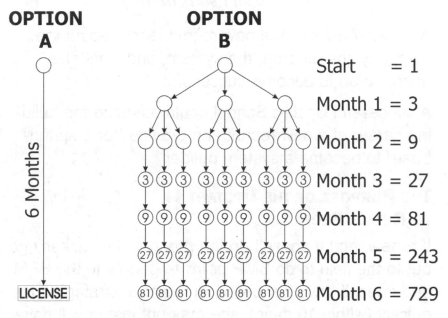

Start = 1
Month 1 = 3
Month 2 = 9
Month 3 = 27
Month 4 = 81
Month 5 = 243
Month 6 = 729

6 Months

LICENSE

- Spend 6 months just to study and get licensed.

- Assuming you recruit just 3 people and help others recruit 3 who recruit 3 per month, in 6 months, you'll have 729 people. At the same time, you study and get licensed.

Which one would you rather have?

| License + 0 team | vs. | License + 729 people |

| No where to go | vs. | Plenty of places to go |

"Can you recruit and get licensed at the same time?"

UPSTART SCHOOL

*"If you don't have a fast start,
you will have a slow start,
or you won't start at all."*

At Upstart School, the new recruit learns about the company, the mission, the system, and what she needs to do to become successful.

A successful Upstart School could advance the building career of a new recruit and provide her a springboard to become a system builder.

THE PURPOSE OF THE UPSTART IS TO RETAIN PEOPLE

If a new recruit doesn't do the prospect list, doesn't go out to the field to do BMP or invite people to the BPM, and doesn't have her personal financial strategy done quickly (within 10 days), she may not last or will have great challenges getting her business off the ground.

> It's difficult to retain people, but it's even more difficult to move people. Most people won't move until they have a track to follow.

A RECRUIT IS NOT A RECRUIT UNTIL SHE HAS A RECRUIT

With a prospect list, the trainer takes the new recruit out to do BMP/BPM, and she may recruit someone. Once she has a recruit under her, she certainly will be excited.

A RECRUIT IS NOT A CRUSADER UNTIL SHE BELIEVES IN OUR MISSION

With the training on our mission, the new recruit understands more about what we can do for the consumer and develops belief in our crusade.

A RECRUIT IS NOT A POTENTIAL BUILDER UNTIL SHE FOLLOWS THE SYSTEM

By doing 1, 2, 3, the recruit begins to systematize, becomes coachable, and follows the system.

ADVANCED PROGRAM

Every two weeks, in concert with Upstart School, many offices run the Advanced Program to train future trainers.

Since there is product training, attendees of the program must submit U-4s and be accepted by the broker dealer. They also need to get licensed fast, so they can go out and practice what they learn.

THE ADVANCED PROGRAM:

1. Provides Proper Time to Train: There are subjects that require more time than the normal BPM training hour. The Advanced Program, which lasts about 4 hours, would provide that time.

2. Allows More Focused Training: In Advanced School, no time is spent on recognition and other BPM protocol.

3. Gives More Confidence to Team Members: Knowledge of our concepts and products will help them understand what we do better.

4. Increases Number of People Who Get Licensed Faster: The extra training helps team members pass their licensing exams.

5. The Crusade-Building Machine: Consistent training prepares team members to offer better service for the client.

MD SCHOOL

"The Baseshop Building Machine"

QUALIFY FOR MD

BUILD A LARGE BASE WITH 10, 15 AND 20 MD CLUBS

MD SCHOOL: THE GIANT BASESHOP BUILDING MACHINE

You cannot build a big team all by yourself. You build it with big building events. The MD school is our giant baseshop building machine.

1. THE MAGIC OF CROWDS

When you have thousands of MD Club qualifiers in one school, you have thousands of "Building Supermen and Superwomen" all under one roof. You alone cannot motivate a MD trainee effectively. But thousands of people can.

2. LEADERSHIP BY EXAMPLE

Every 3 months, the trainee is exposed to great do-it-first leaders whom she can learn from and duplicate. People tend to copy their role models. This is a fast track giant duplication program.

3. COMPETITION

Great team builders are great competitors. A competitive environment revs up the inner drive of the trainee, racing her way to the top.

4. BRING MORE MD CLUB QUALIFIERS

The size of your baseshop depends on the number of MD Club qualifiers inside your base.

5. COMPRESS TIME FRAMES, COMPRESS ACTIVITIES

Instead of waiting for annual events, we compress the frequency of events down to every 3 months. Everybody has an equal opportunity to build faster with this system than with only 1 or 2 events a year.

6. FOCUS ON BUILDING THE BASE

Consistent, relentless focus on the base will ensure long-term success to a new generation of big base-shop builders.

7. PREDICTABLE

The MD School is like a scanning machine that examines the growth or decline of your business. To measure the buildup of future leaders, just count how many MD Club members in your base,

> Think about it: What if you brought 100 MD Club qualifiers to MD School?

superbase, and superteam go to MD School. If you have more MD Club members going to MD School, your team is growing. If you have less, your team is dying. And if you have the same number of MD Club members, your team is stagnating.

8. HERO-MAKING MACHINE

MD School cranks out future leaders by the thousands. It's the Olympic training for future builder athletes.

9. MD CLUB + MD SCHOOL = MD

The main purpose of the MD School is to build a large base with 10 to 20 MD Club members.

A MD Club member who goes to MD School will be inspired and make a decision to become MD.

"Success goes to those leaders who consistently bring more and more people to the MD School."

A SYSTEM OF DISCIPLINE

MD School is a super discipline system. It allows you to recognize who in your team is disciplined enough to stay with you in the long run. If you're in business with us long enough, you'll come to appreciate the fact that we have a system.

Everything we do here requires discipline. It takes a disciplined person to go out in the field during the evening. And it takes a super disciplined person to go to the big event.

In our business we have options: you don't have to do the business every night and you don't have to go to the big event. But then you find out by the end of the day, whether you win or lose in life, it's not because you lack talent, capital, or desire. You lack discipline. You lack the things that successful people have. Discipline is the ability to do the things you hate. And that's pretty tough. The things that you don't want to do, that's what you have to do.

Everyday there are a thousand things you don't want to do. In our business, there are a zillion things you won't want to do. Every time you pick up the phone, you don't want to do it. You see that name, and you hate it already. They jacked you around ten times already. But can you discipline yourself to call the eleventh time?

MD: THE NEW SYSTEM BUILDER

1. RECRUITING MENTALITY. A true builder always maintains good recruiting numbers in the base. He must prospect, invite, and do presentations consistently to cultivate the habits of a recruiting mentality.

2. BUILDER'S MINDSET. The System Flow systematizes the MD Factory. By running the recruiting machine, the MD Club, and the MD School, the new recruit is on track to develop a builder's mindset.

"You don't build a MD.
You build a recruiting and building machine."

3. MEETING MENTALITY. Every few months, the MD School builds a new wave of MD Club members to become big baseshop builders. In turn MD Club members bring new MD Club qualifiers to the next MD School. In effect, the MD becomes a director of motivation. Thus, through the MD school, the MD achieves the meeting mentality, which is the backbone of our business.

4. LEADING BY EXAMPLE. Manage activities, but focus on results. The MD is a do-it-first leader. He runs the system, recruits, builds, and motivates. The MD is the recruiting fireball of the business.

MD FACTORY

"The Hierarchy/Outlets Building Machine"

QUALIFY FOR EXECLUB
3 DIRECT MDs

EXECLUB MEMBER
BE COACHED BY SYSTEM
BUILDERS TO BECOME
CEO-MD AND BUILD A
LARGE TEAM OF MDs

BUILD 3 MDS

"Execlub is the threshold of big builders."

Immediately after you become MD, you must work hard to qualify for Execlub. You need to build your first 3 MDs.

The common trap of many newly promoted MDs is to learn the role of the MD. Just like the young man who just moves out of his parents' house and is preoccupied with all the new things for the new apartment, young MDs try to set up the office, do paperwork, learn to run the baseshop, learn to run the show. These tasks may set them back or slow them down greatly.

BUILD MDs

As a new MD your main focus should be to quickly identify 3 potential MDs-to-be in your base. As you work relentlessly with these people and help them become MD, you develop the skills of a builder.

> **Building your first MD is the hardest. The next won't be as difficult.**

EXECLUB

*"It's hard to build a big base.
But it's even harder to build a big hierarchy."*

Most builders have great challenges building and maintaining a big hierarchy. That's why a lot of people cease to grow once they achieve a certain level.

1. YOUR ULTIMATE GOAL IS TO BECOME THE LEADER OF THOUSANDS

If you grow a little backyard garden, you can do it yourself. But if you want to have a big farm, you need help. Likewise, if you want to build a big hierarchy, you need coaching.

The Execlub is an attempt to provide future giant builders a breeding ground for growth, a haven from being trapped by their own small team.

For you to grow, you need to align yourself with someone bigger than you. Otherwise, your team's potential will be limited by your own potential.

"It's hard to show someone how to do things bigger than you. It's hard to show someone how to make more money than you."

Everybody needs coaching, whether a brand new trainee, a field leader, a MD, or even a CEO. Having a good coach boosts your confidence and your team's confidence.

2. BE PART OF A WINNING TEAM

When you're in a team of great builders, your chances of winning increase tenfold. This is the secret to the success of our business. In the industry, there are a lot of good people, but they tend to play their lonely game. It's difficult to find any big builders in the industry, and if there are, they probably don't work together.

"Our goal is to help builders be in business for themselves but not build by themselves."

3. BUILDERS BUILD BIGGER TOGETHER

The network of Execlub leaders provides sideline motivation and cooperation to build long-distance. It's a great way to build multiple baseshops in multiple locations. This is a perfect example of teamwork on a high level.

4. THE BIGGER YOU ARE THE MORE COACHABLE YOU SHOULD BE

There's no better way to demonstrate the greatness of a leader than by showing that he's a good follower, a coachable team member.

5. HOW MANY LEADERS IN YOUR TEAM QUALIFY FOR EXECLUB?

Wouldn't you want your CEO to take care of your leader and free up your time to go out, recruit and build more of them?

COACHABLE VS. TEACHABLE

Ability to Follow	Ability to Learn
Follower	Student of the Business
Stumble Forward	Understand the Reason
Fire Up w/ Emotion	Justify w/ Logic
Strategic Move	Tactical Execution
Tell Them	Show Them
Order	Instruct

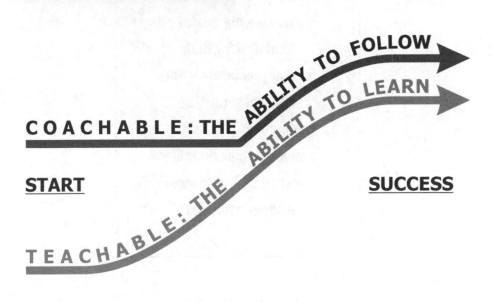

COACHABLE: THE ABILITY TO FOLLOW

TEACHABLE: THE ABILITY TO LEARN

START   SUCCESS

When you start, you don't know a lot. You need a ton of coachability. In the first few years, be totally coachable, follow your leader, and follow the system. Align yourself with our successful system builders.

You should always be coachable. You should always be teachable. You should always keep growing.

> Eventually, when people begin to learn and accumulate knowledge and experience, they think they know a lot. They become uncoachable too soon and end up making big mistakes that destroy their career prematurely and unnecessarily. The minute most MDs get promoted, they do things on their own, and most struggle after that.

"Coach them first.
Teach them after.
Do it first, and you will learn."

THE MIGHTY FORCE OF HABIT

*"The individual who wants to
reach to the top in business
must appreciate the might of the force
of habit—and must understand that
practices are what create habits.
He must be quick to break those habits
that can break him—and hasten to
adopt those practices that will become
the habits that help him achieve
the success he desires."*

— J. PAUL GETTY

YOU ARE A PRODUCT OF YOUR ENVIRONMENT

A lot of times you handicap yourself by limiting yourself to the standards of other builders. You do yourself a disservice.

What's the dangerous game of comparison? When people compare, do they compare themselves to the highest standard or the lowest? They often follow the lowest. Too bad some of you compare yourself to the lowest of the low.

Imagine you are in an office where people make two sales a month, and because you make four sales a month, people say, "Man, you're a hero." Then by that standard, you're trapped.

But let's say you're in an environment where making one sale a day is normal, and thirty sales a month is the norm. The day you don't make a sale you feel bad.

A bunch of guys in my office start acting like the people around them. That's where they're dead. You go to my office, and you always see a lot of people sitting around.

This MD is in front of the computer, the next MD is in front of the computer, and you look at the MD across and he's also on the computer, so you want to be on the computer. When you get to the office, you're dead on arrival.

You box yourself in the situation. Did you know you are what environment you're in? Whatever environment you're in, you are what you are.

Every one of you dies from your own environment. Unless you change the environment. Did you know that if one guy in the office talks about the wrong product, the whole office is dead? Just one guy. Do you know that only one guy needs to have a flu to infect everybody?

If you do not understand the power of The System Flow and you are not using it properly, the minute you go back to your office and revert to the same mode, then you're dead. You walk in your office with the same standards, and you're totally dead.

Unless you get out of your box. Get out of the box.

CR

MD FACTORY: A SYSTEM WHEREBY BUILDING MDS NEVER STOP

BUILD MDs:

Every MD Trainee qualifies for MD Club.

Every MD Club member qualifies for MD.

Every MD qualifies for Execlub.

> **CREATE A PIPELINE**
>
> **MD Trainee ⇨ MD Club ⇨ MD ⇨ Execlub**

BUILD HIERARCHY:

Every MD must set a goal on the number of MDs they are going to build.

> **TARGET SPEED:**
>
> **"Double your MDs every 3 months."**
>
> — XUAN'S MD LAW

By running the MD Club / MD Factory, you can build an incredible number of MDs in just one year.

If you have 2 MDs in January:

You may have 4 MDs by April,

       8 MDs by July (target CEO),

       16 MDs by October,

       32 MDs by the end of the year.

RECRUITING

*The secret of success is not in
your luck or talent.
It is in having many talented
people working with you or
for you.
You have a chance to bring
in not only hundreds but
thousands of people working
in your organization.
This is where ordinary people
can do extraordinary things.
Focus on recruits.
Your dreams can come true.*

RECRUITING MENTALITY

It's hard to describe a "mentality," or a recruiting mentality. For the more I try to describe it, the more I deviate from the real meaning. In French, they say, *"Traduire, c'est trahir,"* which means to translate is to betray.

For example, how do you define "love"? Can you explain "a song"? Can you see "air"? Can you show "water" to the fish? Can you describe a "river" or "the Mississippi"? How about what it means to be "a parent"?

You probably never can. You can talk about it. You can hear of some experience about it. But you would never fully know it until you live through it and live with it.

RECRUITS ARE THE LIFELINE OF YOUR BUSINESS

No recruits and your organization dies, like a body lacking air. Without recruits, there will be no BPMs, no BMPs, no meetings, no field training, no sales, no money, no promotions, no hope, no dreams, and no mission. Without recruits, you're in a state of coma.

RECRUITING IS A STATE OF URGENCY AND EMERGENCY!

"Business opportunity and a sense of urgency always go together."

How about a "gambler's mentality"? The gambler has a gambling mentality. He is totally focused. He can sit for hours, even days, without tiredness or distraction. He puts everything he's got on the line. He's in the game.

What about a recruiter's mentality? Do we have the same intensity?

1. You Must Be Excited

◆ Set yourself on fire (with enthusiasm), and when people come to watch you burn, recruit them.

◆ 90% of recruiting is being excited. Nobody would listen to or follow a non-excited person.

◆ Excitement creates curiosity. Enthusiasm breeds confidence.

> *"Either you infect them with your enthusiasm*
> *and inject them with your crusade,*
> *or they will reject and eject you."*

◆ Your excitement comes from the belief in our mission of doing great things to help people and the faith that you will win.

2. You Must Be in a Hurry

◆ You must always be on the run.

◆ When you talk on the phone, don't sit. Stand up. Walk around. Smile.

◆ When you drop by, tell them that you only have limited time, that you must get to the next appointment soon, that you won't be there long.

◆ When you do the BPM, tell them you wish you had more time. This thing moves fast.

◆ When you talk to your team, tell them you can't wait to run.

> *"If you can run and smile at the same time,*
> *you understand recruiting."*

YOU'D BETTER BE RUNNING

Every morning, a gazelle wakes up.

It knows it must run faster

than the fastest lion or it will be killed.

Every morning, a lion wakes up.

It knows it must outrun the slowest gazelle

or it will starve to death.

It doesn't matter whether you are a lion

or a gazelle: when the sun comes up,

you'd better be running!

– AFRICAN PROVERB

THE LAW OF AVERAGES AND THE LAW OF LARGE NUMBERS

You must observe the laws of nature. For example, according to the law of gravity, every object you drop will gravitate toward the center of the Earth.

THE LAW OF AVERAGES AND THE LAW OF LARGE NUMBERS APPLY TO RECRUITING

If you flip a coin 1 time, you may get 1 head or 1 tail. If you flip a coin 3 times, you may get all 3 heads or all 3 tails. But if you flip a coin 10 times or more, you definitely will get some heads and some tails.

> **MORE TALK = MORE RECRUITS**
>
> **NO TALK = NO RECRUITS**

Likewise, if you talk to 1 person, you may get a Yes or a No. If you talk to 3 people, you may get all 3 Nos or all 3 Yeses. But if you talk to 10 people or more, you will get some Yeses and some Nos.

Many new recruits talk to 3 or 4 friends who say No to them and unfortunately give up too early.

YOU HAVE TO TALK TO MANY PEOPLE MANY TIMES

Even if you only talk to one person, talk to him many times. If you talk to him 1 time, he may say No. If you talk to him 3 or 4 times, he may still say No. But if you keep talking, he may say Yes someday.

It's a numbers business. The more you talk, the more you contact, the more chances you'll have of getting a Yes.

RECRUIT: HOW OR WHY?

*"If you have a big enough why,
you will figure out how."*

One of the most frequently asked questions in this business is: "How do I recruit?"

We have classes and training on how to do PPL, how to make phone calls, how to drop by, how to do a BMP, how to invite, etc. But all of these "How to" sessions don't matter much. Maybe 10%.

If you want to be successful doing something, especially recruiting, you don't need to know how. You need know why.

RECRUITING IS 90% WHY AND ONLY 10% HOW

For example: If we decide to make a "special offer" that if anyone recruits 10 people in 30 days, we will promote them to MD. If this is the case, most people will qualify for MD this month. In fact, some of them will qualify in a few days.

So although people may not know how yet, the reason why–to become a MD–was so strong they would go out and do it, whether they knew how or not.

Another example: Let's say we "guarantee" an income of $100,000 per year if you personally recruit 5 people each month for the next 12 months. If that were true, there would be a long line of people signing up for this job.

WHY DO YOU DO THIS BUSINESS?

Write down the top 10 reasons why you do this business. Write down the things you want to accomplish so badly in your life—the reasons that will change your life and the lives of your loved ones, reasons like providing for your kids, buying your dream home, or taking your parents on a vacation of a lifetime.

One of my top 10 reasons when I joined the business was to retire my wife from her job, something I wanted to do since we got married. I was able to achieve this goal 2 years after I joined the business.

If these reasons are really important to you, you will prospect, you will recruit, you will do whatever it takes to succeed. All the Nos won't affect you much because your reason to go on is strong.

> *"If the reason is strong enough,*
> *you'll find a way."*

TOP 10 REASONS

Write down your top 10 reasons why you do this business and read them everyday—every morning when you wake up and every night before you go to sleep. Do it until you achieve your goal.

I do this business because:

1. _____

2. _____

3. _____

4. _____

5. _____

6. _____

7. _____

8. _____

9. _____

10. _____

RECRUITS SOLVE ALL PROBLEMS OF THE BUSINESS

- ▶ When you have no appointments, RECRUIT!
- ▶ When you have no money, RECRUIT!
- ▶ When you have no momentum, RECRUIT!
- ▶ When you are frustrated with your team, RECRUIT!
- ▶ When your team doesn't recruit, RECRUIT!
- ▶ When your team doesn't sell, RECRUIT!
- ▶ When your team complains, RECRUIT!
- ▶ When your team loses the dream, RECRUIT!
- ▶ When your team has no excitement, RECRUIT!
- ▶ When your team misses a meeting, RECRUIT!
- ▶ When the market drops, RECRUIT!
- ▶ When somebody quits, RECRUIT!
- ▶ When your big guy disappears, RECRUIT!
- ▶ When you're down, RECRUIT!
- ▶ When you think about your family, RECRUIT!
- ▶ When you want to help somebody, RECRUIT!
- ▶ When you want to be somebody, RECRUIT!
- ▶ When you have to be at a party, RECRUIT!
- ▶ When you go shopping, RECRUIT!
- ▶ When your car breaks down, RECRUIT!
- ▶ When you get a traffic ticket, RECRUIT!
- ▶ When you go to the dentist, RECRUIT!
- ▶ When you want to win, RECRUIT!
- ▶ When your team wants to win, RECRUIT!

YOU RECRUIT AND RECRUIT AND RECRUIT!

RECRUIT QUANTITY

"One recruit a day keeps poverty away."

1. RECRUIT THE WARM MARKET

◆ Recruit people you know well: your friends, relatives, co-workers, and neighbors.

◆ Your natural market helps you get started. You can quickly get your top 25 names in this market, qualify the first 5, and drop by to do BMP, or invite them to the BPM.

◆ You can recruit 3 in the first 7 days to qualify for MD Club. That is the minimum. You should do more than that.

> *"Your warm market is sometimes not that warm.*
> *They can give you a lot of negativity,*
> *and you tend to take it personally!"*

Remember: It's just the beginning. Nobody relies on just friends and family to build a business, any business, for the long term. So don't get so cold by your warm market.

2. LUKEWARM MARKET

◆ Recruit acquaintances and referrals: people you meet, people you come across everyday, people you do business with, your customers, the salesperson, a friend of a friend, the technician across the hall, etc.

◆ You may know hundreds of these people. You can also get referrals from people you know. These people are the backbone of your prospect list. This is the market that you go to work with everyday. Add new names to the prospect list, make contact, build relationships, send a brochure, or drop off a video.

◆ The prospect lists of your teammates are also from the lukewarm market. With these lists, you should never run out of places to go or people to call.

*"The lukewarm market is
an endless source of prospects."*

3. COLD MARKET

◆ You can recruit strangers: by looking up people on a telephone list, knocking on people's doors, running into people at the shopping mall, anybody. But of course, it's cold. The odds of recruiting these people are slim. But then again, you never know. I came from the cold market. The person who recruited me met me cold in a building hallway.

*"The warm market can be very cold,
and the cold market can sometimes be very warm."*

THE MARKET IS READY FOR A RECRUITING EXPLOSION
Baby Boomers

There are 76 million baby boomers in the United States. Most are in their 50's. Retirement is around the corner. Many of them are dying for a solution. Many have been laid off, some several times. Many have jobs they don't like. But they don't want to be

Please note that our system is not doing well with the cold market. So don't bank on it. It puzzles me to see people prospect the cold market while they have many people in the warm and lukewarm markets untouched!

recruited. They need somebody who cares and shows them a solution. Show them your belief. Show them this is something different.

Generation X

Gen Xers are in their 30s and 40s. For many the handwriting is on the wall. Maybe they were laid off. Maybe they have the wrong job and are looking for a way out. Most of them do not like to go to a meeting or a seminar, but they're willing to listen if you care enough to come to their place.

The Young Generation

Most young people are smart. Many of them don't want to make the same mistakes of the older generation. A lot of young people nowadays know they want to be in business.

The Employed: They should consider a second career.

The Unemployed: They definitely need to see a new career.

The Underemployed: This can be the answer for them.

The Ambitious: Our opportunity will give them a chance to be big.

Dissatisfied: We can show them the way out.

The Financial Industry: They may want to be in a better team and a better company with a better system.

The Non-Financial Industry: They should definitely look into our wonderful industry.

The Professional and the Entrepreneur: They cannot miss the best business potential of a lifetime.

The Day Shifter - the Night Shifter - the Odd Hours Shifter: They should shift to a no-shift career. They can take control of their time. The only thing they need to do is to shift to a higher gear in their life.

The Desperate: This business can give them hope.

The Confused: This can be the system that they can follow.

The Dreamer and the Mover and Shaker: They can build it big, impact tens of thousands of people, and make a difference in the world.

The Men and Women on a Mission: This is something to believe in.

The Unrecognized and Unappreciated: Here they can be somebody. They can be proud and successful. They can be on top of the world.

The Excited: This will fit their character.

The Shy: After awhile most of them overcome their shyness and gain confidence.

The Highly Educated: They won't be trapped by their degree.

The Less Educated: They won't be handicapped by their lack of education. Here they earn through their effort, not by their I.Q.

The Optimistic: They want to help people.

The Worried: They can build something solid and secure.

The Risk Taker: How big can they build?

The Timid: We will be there for them.

The Strong: This will test their strength and leadership ability.

The Weak: Here, we work together as a team.

The Married: They should do this for their family.

> **PRIORITY OF RECRUITING**
>
> **RECRUIT YOURSELF FIRST,**
>
> **RECRUIT YOUR SPOUSE,**
>
> **THEN RECRUIT THE WORLD.**

Single: They have plenty of time.

The Salespeople: Can they sell the business? Can they sell something bigger?

The People Afraid of Selling: We just share information.

People Who Like Change: This could be the best change they could make.

People Who Don't Like Change: Life will change them anyway. May as well do it now.

The Rich: They could set a good example and share what they know.

The Poor: It's time they made some real money.

The Middle American: They should make a difference for others, for their family and for their life.

"Let's recruit the world!"

RECRUIT THE QUALITY MARKET

RECRUIT THE 7 POINTERS:

1. Over 25 years old
2. Married
3. Children
4. Income
5. Homeowner
6. Ambitious
7. Dissatisfied

Your chances of winning are better with "quality" people because people know people like themselves.

IF THEY'RE YOUNG, THEY WILL RECRUIT YOUNG PEOPLE

People who are less than 25 years old are likely in school or just finished with college. They have a different focus. Education is probably their first priority, as are finding a job and starting up their life. Not to mention they probably have a relationship and are preparing for marriage.

Most young recruits come and go. They normally are very excited and bring in a lot of people. But later on, they can't sell, most of their market is young, they don't have money, and they don't have urgent needs. Many end up not getting licensed either.

IF THEY'RE TOO OLD, THEY ARE OFTEN BUSY WITH ALL KINDS OF COMMITMENTS

They're not easily excited like the young people.

They're very conservative. Many have been shafted by their boss or their co-workers.

When they go out to recruit their friends and relatives, it's the most difficult market to break into. Most people tell them it's too late, and they probably agree with them.

IF THEY'RE IN THE POOR MARKET, THEY WILL RECRUIT PEOPLE FROM THE POOR MARKET

Most of them have no money. They can barely survive. How can they think about saving or investing? Many lack confidence. Poor people are also too busy making ends meet.

IF THEY'RE TOO RICH, THEY MAY NOT NEED OUR OPPORTUNITY

If they are already financially independent, they may be too comfortable and satisfied to start a new career.

THAT IS THE REASON WE WANT TO LOOK FOR THE QUALIFIED MARKET

People who are over 25 and married with kids and who own a home have a lot of responsibility. They have needs to protect their family, to save for their kids' education, and to invest long term for their retirement, and they may have some disposable income to do it. They know people like them, too. They want to make money, but they begin to face reality. Their job won't help them achieve security or prosperity. And they have great motivation: their spouse, their kids, their parents, their hope to be somebody.

THE 8TH POINT: COACHABLE

"Coachability: The true quality factor."

For many years, whenever I recruited people, I always wanted to look for the quality recruit. I understood that I must recruit a lot of people, that I shouldn't prejudge people, and that my superstar could be anybody. "As long as I keep recruiting tons of people," I told myself, "I would find somebody who wants it as bad as I do." And I did find quite a few.

After recruiting thousands, I found that the first 5 points were important but not that important, because I recruited a lot of people who had the first 5 points, the people in the "good market," but they still died out of the business as fast as the ones who had fewer points.

THE 7 POINTERS

1. 25+ years old
2. Married
3. Children
4. Homeowner
5. Income
6. Ambitious
7. Dissatisfied

Then I discovered that the 6th pointer is more important than the first 5 because it doesn't matter whether they're in the "right market". If they're not ambitious, there's not much we can do for them. If they are not hungry, if they have no desire, if they do not want to be big, they won't do anything.

Later I discovered another surprise. There are many people in the "right market" who have ambitions but still fail in the business. It's the 7th pointer–dissatisfied–which is key, because it doesn't matter if they are ambitious or if they want to be successful. If they're already happy with their current situation, if they're content with their job and they have good income, they won't do anything either.

Unless their back is against the wall, unless they're so unhappy about their situation, unless they're sick and tired of being sick and tired, unless they have a high level of frustration… they won't do anything. Ever since I had that realization, I didn't care about any other qualities. I just looked for the ambitious and the dissatisfied. So with all my effort, I paid special attention to these people.

But even these people still die! I was miserable! How can these people–who have the right qualities, who say they want it bad, who say they hate their jobs–how can so many of them fail?

Finally, I got a rude awakening: They were uncoachable. Again, it didn't matter that they had all the qualities of the "right" person. If they're not coachable, they die just as fast as any other.

Many of these men and women look like a million bucks. They look right. They say the right things. But they're too impressed with themselves. The minute they start, they question, they demand, but they don't want to listen.

They do things their way. They come when they want. They leave when they want. They seem to be busy or have something more important happening all the time. But they keep telling me they want it bad! They give me hope one day and disappointment the next. They put me through an emotional roller coaster.

Ultimately, I discovered the true factor of success. In just about every successful builder whom I have had a chance to work with, I found that they are very coachable. Many of them don't even have 2 or 3 points. At first glance, they may look like they're from the wrong market. They look very simple, very average, but deep down they're hungry, they're dissatisfied, they're willing to listen, to learn, and to try. And that makes all the difference.

THE 8 POINTERS

Now, the first quality I look for is point number 8. Without coachability, the whole system collapses. In a system, you must follow what's necessary to make the system work.

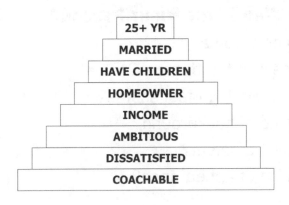

"Coachability is the #1 quality of a system builder."

RECRUIT QUANTITY TO GET QUALITY

"If you judge people,
there is no time to love them."
— MOTHER THERESA

If you prejudge people, you may not take the time to get to know them.

Who you should recruit, who you should work with, is always the big question in our business. However, there are 3 problems to finding the right person.

◆ **Problem #1:** You are not a fortune teller. You cannot predict who will be the right person for the business.

◆ **Problem #2:** You are not God. You cannot say, "This person deserves the opportunity and that person doesn't." You have no right to deny a man or a woman the chance to be somebody.

◆ **Problem #3:** You are not a boss who hires a person based on a resume. This is not corporate America.

SO THEN WHO IS THE RIGHT PERSON?

◆ A man or a woman?
◆ The one with the degrees?
◆ The one with high test scores?
◆ What kind of background?
◆ What kind of talent?
◆ What kind of appearance?

It Is Impossible to Prejudge a Winner by His or Her Appearance or Background

You cannot judge a book by its cover. There is no way you can tell if a person can make it until you give them a chance. In fact, almost all predictions turn out to be wrong.

There is no such thing as a small guy or a big shot. You never know. A lot of simple-looking people turn out to be superstars, while a lot of big shots turn out to be big flops.

By the way, what's a "quality" person anyway? A quality person should be judged by their work ethic, by their character, by the way they treat others, and by the way they live their life—not by their degrees, wealth, looks, or background.

Although in earlier chapters we do talk about looking for the 7 pointers—25+ years, married, kids, income, home, ambitious, dissatisfied—this suggestion has no basis in finding winners. It just suggests a defined market.

You Must Recruit Quantity to Get Quality

From a large number of people, the winners will rise up. That's why you must recruit a lot of people. You have better odds of finding good builders among 100 recruits than among 10.

MORE RECRUITS = MORE WINNERS

LESS RECRUITS = LESS WINNERS

NO RECRUITS = NO WINNERS

DON'T PICK A WINNER TOO EARLY

Some people recruit a person with 6 or 7 points and think they found a superstar. Don't celebrate too soon. It's impossible to know. In fact, someone who comes in and explodes right away may not last, while somebody else who struggles in the early years can turn out to be the toughest and the strongest in the long run.

"This is a business of desire, discipline, character, and endurance. This is a test of will, not skill. Anybody can be a winner."

RECRUIT THE LOW HANGING FRUIT

"Two men with the same basket went to an apple farm. The first picked the apples within his reach and moved fast from one tree to the next. The other was more choosy. He looked for the right size, color, and look. He even found a ladder to climb up to pick the ones up high. After a while the first one had his basket full, while the second one was still barely getting a few apples."

RECRUIT UP, NOT DOWN

"It's easier to recruit down."

Most people tend to recruit "down". For example, you recruit a manager, the manager recruits the engineer, the engineer recruits the technician, the technician recruits the production line worker, and finally the production line worker recruits the janitor.

However, things that look easy may not turn out to be that easy. Once you head into the wrong market, it's hard to build further. If that's so, then what's left for you to recruit?

The good news is that you have plenty of quality market. There are a lot of people in the quality market out there looking for help and for an opportunity.

Also, people who seem to be in the wrong market may not be the wrong recruit after all. There are a lot of successful builders who come from the young, single market. There are also people from very poor backgrounds as well as people from very wealthy backgrounds who become successful in our business.

MOVE LIKE WATER

"The army's disposition of force is like water. Water's configuration avoids heights and races downward. The army's disposition of force avoids the substantial and strikes the vacuous. Water configures its flow in accord with the terrain; the army controls its victory in accord with the enemy. Thus, the army does not maintain any constant strategic configuration of power. Water has no constant shape."

— SUN TZU

You know why we call it The System Flow? Because it flows. Anything that works so hard won't flow.

Keep flowing. Move like water. Water doesn't try so hard, but it flows. When water hits a rock, it avoids the rock and goes around it. Water sees the high land and never tries to climb it. Water takes the low road. That's how water flows.

This is also how you do the business, you always got to keep moving. If people don't join, move on. If people don't buy, move on. If people don't want to build, move on.

Don't hit your head against the wall trying to convince the rock to buy, to join, or to do something it doesn't want to do. Just move on.

RECRUITING MINDSET

"Believe that life is worth living and your belief will help create the fact."

— WILLIAM JAMES

- ◆ This is a breakthrough.

- ◆ I'm so lucky.

- ◆ I believe in this business.

- ◆ This is my way out.

- ◆ This is my wake-up call.

- ◆ I can do it.

- ◆ This is the time.

- ◆ It's proven.

- ◆ What an incredible system.

- ◆ What a powerful concept.

- ◆ What a historic moment.

- ◆ This is the future.

"Don't recruit people. Show them your belief."

THE EMOTIONAL CONNECTION

"People react to emotion."

LOGIC OR EMOTION?

Whenever we make decisions, we tend to calculate the pros and cons. We use our logic to evaluate the calories in a meal, the capacity of a computer, the features of a car. We compare shoes, shirts, and pants by feeling the material, looking at the color, and finding the right size. We're very logical, it seems.

But in fact, most of the time, we are not so logical. When we go shopping, we intend to buy a shirt but end up with a suit. We stick to a diet for the whole day but end up with a big dessert. We intend to buy a Toyota but drive home with a Lexus. We buy all sorts of things we never use, like expensive shoes that are rarely worn or options in the car that are never used.

That's why the salesperson at the department store says, "You look so good in that suit. This color makes you look so much younger!" The salesperson's not going to tell you, "This suit costs $1,000!"

Most of us react with our feelings and emotions more often than with our logic. Hey, we're human.

Thus, when doing this business, we must always understand the mighty force of emotion. When we get connected or affected by something, we will make decisions about it. Our job is to get the client involved, to take the issue that is important to them seriously. Our job also is to make them understand these issues, so that they can make the right decision for their life.

EMOTION CREATES MOTION

*"When we get so excited
about something,
we will jump into it.
When we get so disappointed
about something,
we will quit doing it.
When we care so much
about something,
we will take care of it."*

When you want your prospect, your client, or your team member to do something, don't talk logic. Get into their heart.

Logically, most people would recruit 1 person a month. But when they're on fire, they recruit 10 people a week.

LOGIC		EMOTION
Don't want to recruit	*but*	Want to be Marketing Director
Don't want to sell	*but*	Want to be on a mission
Don't want to do PPL	*but*	Want to help people they know
Don't want a second career	*but*	Want to be financially independent
Don't want to join	*but*	Want to invest their time
Don't want to buy	*but*	Want to take care of their family
Don't want a boss	*but*	Want to follow a leader
Don't want to go to the meeting	*but*	Want to experience a life-changing event
Don't want to make money on friends	*but*	Want friends to be successful in business
Don't want to sell to relatives	*but*	Has the responsibility to share what they know
Don't do things for themselves	*but*	Would do it for the team's pride
Don't want to push anyone	*but*	Want them to win
Don't want a shirt	*but*	Want to be recognized
Don't want a system	*but*	Want to be a giant builder

Get into what's important to them emotionally.

MOVE THEM WITH EMOTION BUT BACK IT UP WITH LOGIC

When you sell to people, sell them the responsibility of taking care of their family and the possibility of building wealth for their family's future. At the same time, back it up with facts, figures, and track records. Otherwise, they may make a decision to buy but will cancel when they think it over! On the other hand, you may show the client all the performance results, the portfolio accounts, and the tax advantages, yet never find out what's most important to them. People don't buy a product. They buy that which betters their life. Therefore, make sure that the products fit their needs and are affordable.

Likewise, when you recruit people, you can sell the dream of being somebody and being a crusader. But you must back it up with local examples of success, people who are living their dream. You must also show them a system that can help them do it, a training program that's proven to work. Otherwise their logical mind, or a negative person, will explain how impossible it will be for them.

If you want your team to move, find out their hot buttons. That's why you should ask your team to write down their top 10 reasons why they do this business. So when they're down, you sell them those things.

I do not know many people dying to get a new house, a new car, or a new title. But I know even more people who want to be special, who want to be recognized, and who want to be proud of themselves and make their family proud of them.

You must know your people. You must have true relationships with your people in order for you to help them.

BIG EMOTIONAL EXPERIENCE = BIG CHANGE

Unless people go through some moving emotional experience, they won't change. A person who doesn't have money won't change. But if someone insults his family due to their poverty, that person will do whatever it takes to be successful.

Big events have that magic. Often, when team members sit in a convention and see people win, people who have less talent and less skill, or people who join later than them, it really touches them emotionally, and when they come back, they no longer accept defeat.

RECRUITING VISION

Recruiting and Vision are the same thing.

Recruiting is:

- Having the Vision
- Sharing the Vision

If you see it, then you can share what you see.

Thus, a team member who doesn't recruit or who slows down on recruits may not have a positive vision of the business or his future.

FOCUS ON SALES OR RECRUITS?

What's the difference between our system versus most of the industry?

The industry focuses on sales. We focus on recruits.

Which one is better? You know our preference.

SALE	RECRUIT
Spend time	Invest time
Linear Income	Team Income
Linear Growth	Geometric Growth
Instant Income	Long Term Overrides
Slow Duplication	Faster Duplication
A Select Few	Everybody
Today's Sale	Vision for the Future
Personal Skill	Team Effort
Your Own Market	Recruits'/Team's Market
No System Needed	System is the Key
Hunter	Farmer
Wants High Contract	Wants High Override
Lonely	Member of a Team
Talks about Products	Talks about Building
Buys Leads	Does Prospect List
Mostly Full-Time	Part/Full/All-the-Time
Glass Ceiling	Unlimited Potential
Self Motivated	Team Motivated

IT'S SIMPLE:
The hunter has
to look for
food everyday,
while the farmer
takes time to
breed, feed, plant,
and grow.

We aim for recruits. We focus on building. As the system flows, those who go through this process may join or buy from us based on their own needs and desires. The difference is that we want to work with large numbers of people to open up more outlets.

3 WAYS TO MAKE MONEY

1. Make money through your own effort

2. Make money through other people's effort

3. Make money make money for you

You make money first through your own personal effort, out in the field recruiting, selling, setting the pace, leading by example.

When your team duplicates and follows you, you are able to make money through your team.

And once you begin to accumulate money, your understanding of how money works can help you have money work to build wealth for you.

THE POWER OF DUPLICATION

You can change your career in a very short period of time—as long as you do it first, and you duplicate it to your people. You must have a duplication mentality.

EACH ONE GETS ONE A WEEK

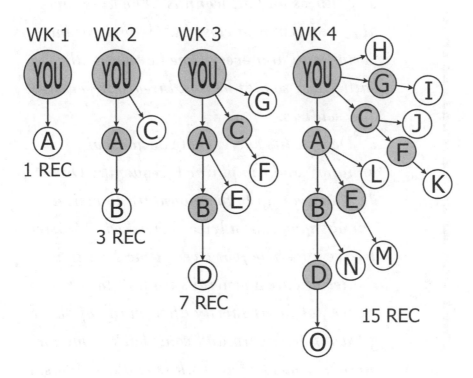

* If you recruit 1 a week and ask every new recruit to do the same, by the fourth week, you'll have 15 recruits.
* If you do the same thing with licensed agents, and each gets 1 sale a week, you'll have a lot of sales.
* If you ask everybody to go get prospect lists, you'll have an explosion.

THE MISERABLE DOCTOR

In old China, there was a great doctor. He was so good that he could cure almost any illness and all wounds. The king loved him and kept him close by. He brought the doctor with him every time he went to the battlefield, so that he could treat his generals and soldiers.

Despite his success, the doctor was unhappy and complained frequently. One day, he went up to the mountain to visit a famous monk for advice. He asked, "Master, I have a terrible job. Every time I treat a soldier or cure a general's wound, they recover. And yet shortly after, many of them get wounded again and come back to me for more treatment. The work is endless. Worst of all, some of the soldiers I treat go back to the battlefield and get killed. The more I do, the more they get hurt, the more they die! Can you help me solve this problem?"

The monk opened his eyes and said, "You're such a stupid doctor. Everyone has a job to do. The soldier's job is to fight for his kingdom. The doctor's job is to treat the wounded. The soldier does his dangerous job without complaints. Why do you complain about doing your job?"

ରେ

BUILDER'S NOTE:

A frequent complaint from many people in the business is: "Why do I have to keep recruiting when they keep dying out of the business? Is there any way I can keep people from quitting?"

You can't change human nature. Like anything in life, people join and quit, whether it's a job, a business, a sports team, or a club. You just keep recruiting. Those who stay will stay. Those who quit will quit.

YOU'RE ONE RECRUIT AWAY FROM AN EXPLOSION

"One recruit equals infinity."

You are always 1 recruit away from an explosion because the minute that recruit decides to work, the potential is unlimited. A fired up recruit will get good prospect lists and do BMPs and BPMs, which create more recruits, and from there anything is possible.

FOR EXAMPLE:

Your 1 Recruit	=	250 Names
250 Names	=	50 BMP/BPMs
50 BMP/BPMs	=	10 Recruits
Her 10 Recruits	=	2,500 Names
2,500 Names	=	500 BMP/BPMs
500 BMP/BPMs	=	100 Recruits
Their 100 Recruits	=	25,000 Names
25,000 Names	=	5,000 BMP/BPMs
5,000 BMP/BPMs	=	1,000 Recruits
Thus, 1 Recruit	=	Infinity

Events too! You're one event away from an explosion. Put popcorn to the fire. When the first one pops, the rest will explode! Bring your team to the big event. They will pop!

BUILDING

There are a lot of great
builders in the world
who build buildings, vehicles,
hardware, software.
We build people.
We change people's lives
as well as our life.
Building a person from
nobody to somebody
is one of the greatest miracles
in this business.
You don't have to change
the world.
First, change your world
then help someone
change their world.

FOUNDATION OF BUILDING
BUILD IT RIGHT, BUILD IT STRONG

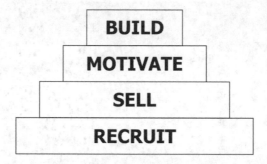

Recruiting is the foundation of building. The sale comes next. Then you motivate your team. Last, you build them to become the leaders of the future.

HOWEVER, MANY PEOPLE DID NOT BUILD IT RIGHT

- Some people recruit a lot yet have few sales.

- Some focus too much on sales and lack recruits.

- Some try so hard to motivate people but forgot to recruit and sell.

- Some keep teaching, training, and building a handful of old people, yet the whole base lacks recruits, sales, and motivation.

WHAT DOES YOUR BASESHOP LOOK LIKE?

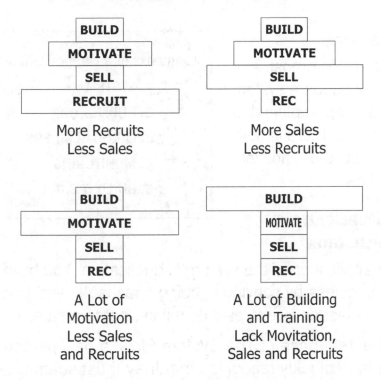

BUILD
MOTIVATE
SELL
RECRUIT

More Recruits
Less Sales

BUILD
MOTIVATE
SELL
REC

More Sales
Less Recruits

BUILD
MOTIVATE
SELL
REC

A Lot of
Motivation
Less Sales
and Recruits

BUILD
MOTIVATE
SELL
REC

A Lot of Building
and Training
Lack Movitation,
Sales and Recruits

A builder's team must always focus on strong recruits and strong sales, only then will motivation and building become possible.

As a leader, you must always maintain a healthy balance and a strong foundation. If the team lacks recruits, you must personally recruit, do PPLs, BMPs, and BPMs to crank up recruiting momentum.

If the team has recruits but ends up with fewer sales, you must work with your trainers to go out in the field, match them up, manage their activities, and follow up on their results.

If you consistently have recruits and sales but produce no leaders and no MDs, you must work on identifying and overlapping leadership to build new potential stars.

A BUILDER'S MINDSET

1. SYSTEM

First and foremost, a builder needs a system, a roadmap, a blueprint. Without it, there is nothing to build on, nothing to follow.

Elements of a Builder's Mind:

1. SYSTEM
2. DUPLICATION
3. LARGE NUMBERS
4. MONITORING
5. BUILD IT BIG

2. DUPLICATION, APPLICATION

The application of the system is duplication. You build this business by copying it, being coachable, and following the leader. You're paid to imitate, not to create.

In the 1st phase of The System Flow, a new person needs to quickly recognize that they must submit U-4 and do 1, 2, 3 in the first 7 days. In the 2nd phase, they qualify for MD Club. In the 3rd phase, they go to MD School. And in the 4th phase, they qualify for Execlub. Everyone does the same.

3. LARGE NUMBERS

This is a numbers business. The builder must have a large-numbers mentality. You don't build one or two people. You build hundreds and thousands of people. You are willing to put in a lot of time and effort to go through large numbers—lots of contact, BMPs, BPMs, hiring interviews, field training, meetings, and conventions.

If you want to build a big castle,
you must have tons of materials.

4. MONITORING

■ Be accountable and responsible. You must monitor, check up, and follow up. Anything you build–whether it's a house, a car, hardware, or software–you must check up on it carefully and regularly or it will break-down. Franchises like McDonald's have strict stan-dards of making sure everyone follows their system.

■ You must also monitor the time frame of comple-tion, how long it takes you to get the job done.

■ You must demand your builders to build it right, build it strong, and build it on time. You must also have strong coaching and strong compliance.

As soon as people join, you expect new members to buy into The System Flow.

- **Start working the system.**
  Prospect, present, recruit, and sell.

- **Expect them to go through many people.**
  Do it again and again.

- **Coach them.** Encourage them.
  Demand them to do it right and to do it big.

5. BUILD IT BIG

It's only worth it if you do it big. You need to have a builder's mindset to build hundreds or thousands of MDs. Otherwise, a handful of MDs can be had through the natural course of time or luck.

BUILD WIDE, DEEP, & BASESHOP: THE FOUNDATION

"You must build at least 5 to 7 strong direct builders."

You don't want to recruit 5 to 7 people. You don't want to have 5 to 7 salespeople. You want to build 5 to 7 builder legs.

You must go through a lot of prospects and recruits and work with them to find these builders.

The only way for you to build wide is to commit to do it personally. Nobody will do it for you. You can't wait for your upline to do it. And you can't wait for your downline to do it.

HOW TO GO WIDE?

You do these relentlessly:

- Prospect
- Contact
- Invite
- Pick prospect up
- Do BMP
- Do BPM
- Make appointments
- Do hiring interview
- Fast start them to MD Club
- PPL them at home
- Do financial strategy (or, if you are not licensed, ask someone licensed to do it)

- Follow up, drop by, call them, remind them, and remind them again

- Then find another person and repeat the same process all over again

You must BMP and BPM consistently. Always have guests, and always do presentations. You keep doing it until you find your first superstar, your first MD, your first builder. Once you get your first, the second will be easier.

Sound like a lot of work? Yes, it is.

BUT:

"What if I'm still new? I don't know how to do the BMP?" Just do it, and you will learn.

> If you wait for your upline to do it for you, prepare to get in line. They have to work on their business too.
> If you wait for your downline to do it, prepare to get disappointed. They're waiting for you. By the way, in any business, nobody expects the higher-ups or the subordinates to do things for them.

"What if I'm scared? I'm afraid to take someone to the BPM?" Just do it, and you won't be scared anymore.

"How to make an appointment?" Just ask.

"Doing the interview? I've never done a recruiting interview in my life!" Just do it. You're the "boss" now. It's your business.

BUILD DEEP

"Every 4 deep, you may get one builder."

Like a tree or a building, unless it goes deep,
it won't stand.

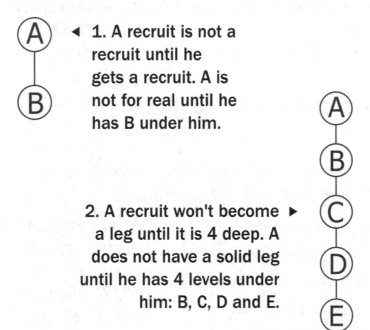

◄ 1. A recruit is not a
recruit until he
gets a recruit. A is
not for real until he
has B under him.

2. A recruit won't become ►
a leg until it is 4 deep. A
does not have a solid leg
until he has 4 levels under
him: B, C, D and E.

WHY 4 DEEP?

RETENTION IS THE MAIN REASON

If you recruit A and A recruits nobody, if A quits, which
happens often, we end up with nothing. But if A
recruits B, A probably won't quit, because he's excited
about having a downline. But even if A does quit, we
still have B left. Same goes for the leg. If you go 4
deep, most likely, all A, B, C, and D will stay because
they have people under them. And even if one or two
of them quit, we will still have enough left to build with.

WIDE AND DEEP

"You go wide to go deep."

GO WIDE TO GO DEEP

You can never go deep by recruiting 1 person.
Thus, you must recruit 3 to 4 wide to find 1 who can
go deep.

4 x 4

Normally, if you go 4 wide, you can find 1 to go 4 deep.

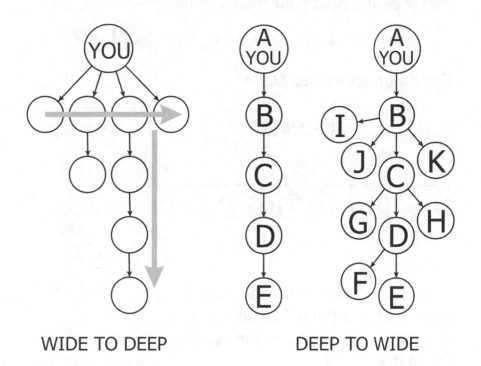

WIDE TO DEEP   DEEP TO WIDE

GO DEEP TO GO WIDE

Assuming you have 4 deep first, you will be wide anyway.

If D has E, D's excited and will get one more person, F.

If C has D, E, and F under him, he will be fired up to get G and H.

If B has C, D, E, F, G, and H, he will be super hot and go wide with I, J, and K.

That's why you should always go wide to go deep and always go deep to go wide. In other words, recruit personal and help your team recruit.

"Since you build anyway, why not build it big?"

FOCUS ON BUILDING DEEP

SCENARIO I   SCENARIO II

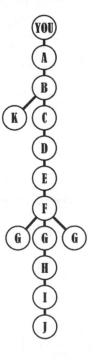

In scenario I, although you have 10 wide, you only have 2 people, C and G, going deep, so the organization is not stable.

In scenario II, everyone in the organization, from A to I, is quite solid because they have someone under them.

Going deep requires the upline to taproot down. This creates a builder's mindset, a recruit-to-build mentality.

DUPLICATION

A never duplicates himself until B can take care of C, D, E, and beyond.

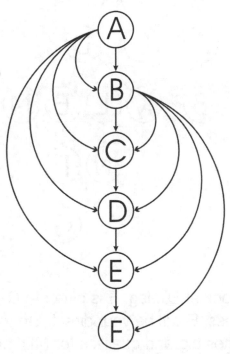

BUILD WIDE FOR PROFITABILITY.

BUILD DEEP FOR LONG TERM SECURITY.

BUILD BASESHOP

"Everybody in the base, wide or deep, is your direct."

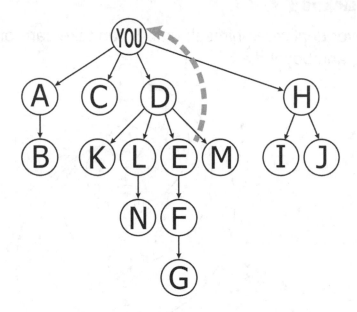

Let's look at D's leg. E is direct to D. But if D quits the business, E will be your direct. On the other hand, if D becomes big and qualifies for MD, and E is the replacement leg, E will eventually be your direct anyway.

So treat everybody in the base as your direct. Don't think that G is too deep under you because he's under F, E, and D. Treat G, F, E like your direct. You work with them, PPL, field train, motivate, build them, and treat everybody the same.

THIS IS THE DYNAMIC OF THE BASE

PICTURE THIS:
The base is like a magic
orange tree that keeps
giving you fruit forever.
It allows you to take off
its branches to trans-
plant new trees. And
every time you take off a
branch, a new branch
suddenly appears to
substitute the old one.

For example: If A is gone, B moves up. If A becomes a
MD, B moves up as a replacement.

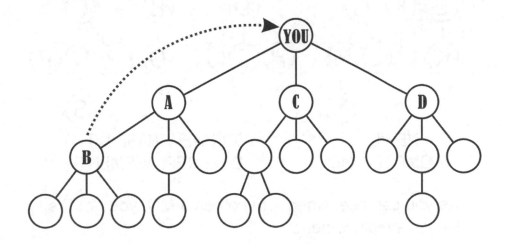

REPLACEMENT

The replacement leg, or exchange leg, makes our system unique. It's the ultimate secret of our success.

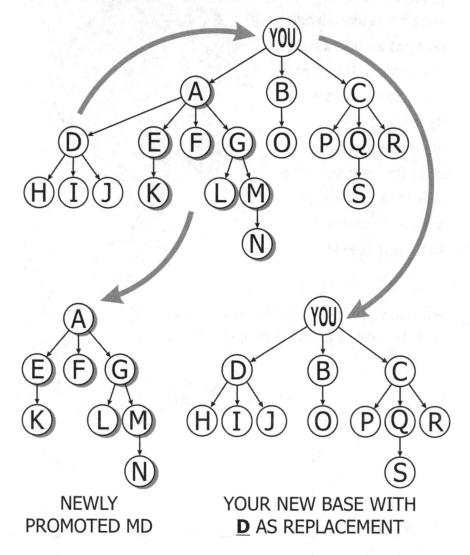

NEWLY
PROMOTED MD

YOUR NEW BASE WITH
D AS REPLACEMENT

As you can see, when A becomes a MD, you get D's leg as a replacement.

IS IT FAIR FOR YOU?

It's fair for you because you recruited A. A knew nothing about the business when he joined. Then you helped A recruit D, E, F, G, H, I, J, K, L, M, N. It's A's team, but it's also your team too.

You built him up. You spent time, money, and a lot of effort for A and all his 4 legs. When he leaves your baseshop to become MD, he still has 3 legs, E, F, G. So it's good for him, and it's good for you.

IS IT FAIR FOR A?

It's fair for A because A will now start building his own base and take replacement legs too.

Let's look at A's new team a few months later on. Assume F and G do nothing, but E grows and explodes.

Now A has a new MD. He's happy to have a 1st generation MD, and he's happy that he has K as a replacement.

The replacement system works the same for everybody. A lost a replacement to you, but he begins to take replacements from all the legs that he will build in the future.

Also note that as A has his first generation MD, E is also your second generation. Isn't that wonderful?

"Replacement, it's a win-win situation.
You exchange one leg. You will receive many."

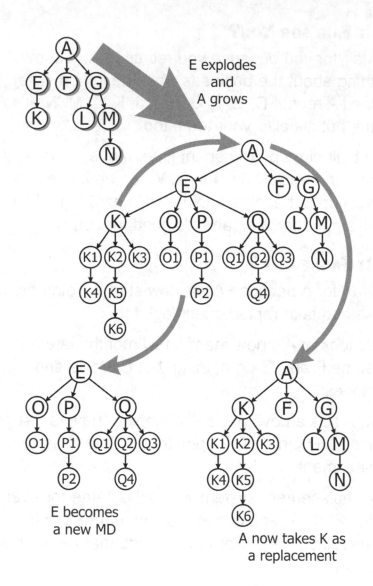

E explodes
and
A grows

E becomes
a new MD

A now takes K as
a replacement

STRONG REPLACEMENT

When you promote a MD, you should take a strong
leg for replacement, so that your baseshop continues
to be strong.

When you become a MD, you should give your upline
your strongest leg, so that you will feel good taking
the strongest leg of your downline later on.

"I'd rather give up 1 strong leg
to get 10 strong legs in the future than give up
1 weak leg to get 10 weak ones.
If you give and take weak replacement legs,
be prepared to deal with a weak,
crippled organization."

BUILD A BIG BASESHOP

"Do it right the first time.
It will last forever.
The future belongs to those
who build big baseshops."

THE BASESHOP IS YOUR BUILDING FOUNDATION

You must build a strong base. Everything about this business depends on how strong you build your base.

Strong Base ⇨ Strong Superbase ⇨ Strong Hierarchy

Weak Base ⇨ Weak Superbase ⇨ Weak Hierarchy

BUILD A MININUM OF 3 STRONG LEGS

Your base should have a minimum of 3 strong legs. This means that you must have a lot more legs. You may need 10 legs to get 3 strong legs.

> What's considered a strong leg? The leg that can produce double-digit recruits and double-digit sales in a month, every month.

THINGS YOU NEED TO DO IN THE BASE

Non-MD Base: Anyone who is not an MD yet, including the person who just joined.

This is very important. If you build a strong non-MD base, you will have a big baseshop. But if you don't do it right, forget about becoming a MD.

Act like a MD now: Too many people keep playing the "I-don't-know, I'm-not-good-enough, I'm-not-ready-yet" game when they start building the business. Everybody has to start somewhere. So did the MD. So why don't you start doing things like her? Do everything the MD does. Only when you are really stuck should you ask her for help.

Prospect, recruit, hire, sell, do paperwork, order supplies, book for conventions, motivate the team, go out of your way to do things and don't expect your upline to do things for your baseshop. You take care of your own base.

MD Base: As an MD, you have a heavy duty:

In my opinion, good recruiting numbers are:

- Average: 25 recruits
- Good: 50 recruits
- Great: 100 recruits

In my opinion, good production is:

- Average: 25 sales / 50K production
- Good: 50 sales / 100K production
- Great: 100 sales / 200K production

Make money: You must make money. Not only for your family, but the base requires you to set a good example of success for the team. You should hit a minimum six-figure annual income.

Go out in the field: It's not an option. You must go out in the field everyday if you want to build the base. The baseshop will collapse if the MD doesn't go out field training.

> You can do anything-BPM, paperwork, training, motivation-but if you don't do field training prospecting, field training recruiting, and field training sales, the base will be crippled.

The environment: The baseshop environment is critical. MoZone must be in motion. There should be no negativity and no distractions. If you share an office with other bases, they must also be positive and must not distract your team.

> **If you share an office with other bases, they must also be positive and must not distract your team.**

The business machine: The purpose of building a base is to build a business machine. Every day, every night, every meeting, sell the business. You sell products to clients, but you sell the business to the team.

The crusade factory: The other purpose of building a base is to create crusaders. We get together as a base to join hands and go out to fulfill our mission as a team. Always do it right, and do it with pride. Do good things for people.

Treat everybody well: Treat your team members and your clients with care and respect. Both have to go together.

Maintain the spirit of the team: If you fail to create teamwork in the base, you will have big trouble later on with the hierarchy. In the people business, everybody is different and tends to do things on their own. Your main job is to build a team. That is when all things become possible.

"Build a team. Sell the dream."

A COMMITMENT TO BUILD

"You must wake up everyday thinking about how to grow your business."

Your ultimate goal is to build a lot of builders. They are the leaders who run a strong baseshop, a strong superbase, and a strong superteam.

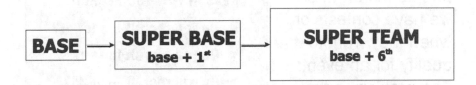

These are your business-es, your outlets, your cash flow machine.

You may recruit a lot, sell a lot, and make good money for now. But if in the future you have no MDs and no builders, you will have wasted your valuable time because you failed to build.

> Three to five years from now, what's your business going to look like? How many MDs or builders will you have in your organization?

Without builders and with-out MDs, you will still have to go to work everyday to make a living. You will have little or no overrides. Nobody is going to work with you or for you.

RECRUIT TO BUILD

1. RECRUIT TO RECRUIT

The emphasis of recruit, recruit, recruit sometimes creates an attitude of recruiting blindly for the purpose of having the maximum number of people join. A lot of people recruit when we have contests or when they want to qualify for an event. The problem is that they do this for the pure purpose of

> **YOU MUST KNOW THE REASON WHY YOU RECRUIT.**
> - **Do you recruit to recruit?**
> - **Do you recruit to sell?**
> - **Do you recruit to build?**

recruiting, and not much happens after that. Other people want to recruit a lot hoping that a superstar will fall from the sky. This is a "network" mentality.

2. RECRUIT TO SELL

When you recruit, the sales will follow. But if that's the only reason you recruit, this kind of thinking is more or less a salesman mentality.

3. RECRUIT TO BUILD

The main purpose of recruiting is neither to recruit nor to sell but rather to build outlets, to build MDs, to build builders.

Therefore, you recruit to build and run the system. Then more recruits and more sales will result from your building efforts.

LADDER OF FOCUS

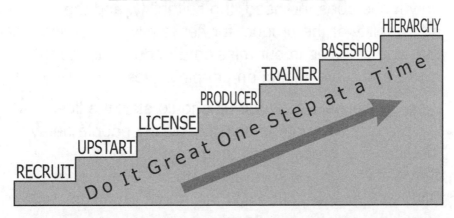

Step 1: Recruit: A new recruit is a great starting point, but it won't be of any good unless the new recruit follows this ladder of focus with urgency.

Step 2: Upstart: A new recruit must accomplish steps 1, 2, and 3–the prospect list, BMP + BPM, financial strategy–within the first 7 days of joining to attend Upstart School as well as qualify for MD Club.

This fast start is so critical for the new person:

> *"A recruit is not for real*
>
> *until she finishes the upstart and*
>
> *qualifies for MD Club."*

A recruit must do PPL to develop her market. She must go out and do a BMP and invite people to the BPM to learn the business, sell the dream, and recruit people. She must sit down with a licensed trainer who will show her how money works, and analyze her family's financial situation, so she can see how we

can help her as well as how we can help the consumer out there. She should make a decision to buy
only if she sees the need, the suitability, and the
affordability of the product for her family. It is critical
that she believes in our mission and our crusade to
make a positive impact on people's lives.

Step 3: License: A new recruit should start the licensing process as soon as possible. Many people delay
the licensing process and drag it on too long.
Sometimes it takes several months or even years.
Without a license, she can't talk about products, make
sales, or make money. Most people who are slow in
this step rarely survive the business. Lack of focus
and lack of desire are the main problems.

On the other hand, there is a reverse problem when
someone comes in, just focuses on licensing, doesn't
want to go through steps 1, 2, 3, won't go to Upstart
school, and has no team. These people skip the
system and hardly make it because what can someone do when they have a license but no recruits, no
prospects, and no understanding of the system?

Step 4: Producer: A good producer makes 4 to 10
sales a month and makes good money on a part-time
basis.

Step 5: Trainer: If the trainee is a good producer,
chances are she can be a good trainer too. However,
if she is a good producer but not a good trainer,
she cannot duplicate herself. Good trainers will train
the trainers that will build the foundation of a big
baseshop.

A good trainer is not just good in making sales. A good trainer is someone who can take a new trainee out to help them do BMP/BPM, present the financial concepts and the PFS, and close the sale. In short, a good trainer can duplicate herself.

Step 6: Baseshop Builder: The baseshop is where everything happens. This is where she starts building a recruiting, building, and motivation factory that trains, shapes, and molds future producers, future trainers, and future baseshop builders.

Step 7: Hierarchy Builder: As she maintains and builds a big baseshop, she will promote new MDs coming out of her base. She needs to build a strong front line. Strong first generation MDs will help her build a big hierarchy.

1. A recruit is not a recruit until she fast starts to the Upstart and MD Club.

2. An upstart without a license will be useless and lose momentum. A licensed person without upstart has no foundation and will usually have no place to go.

3. A licensed person must become a good personal producer and make money.

4. A good producer sharpens her skill to become a good trainer.

5. A good trainer will be able to train new people and duplicate herself.

6. Good trainers build big baseshops.

7. Big baseshop builders build big hierarchies.

DON'T BE A REGULAR BUILDER, BE A SYSTEM BUILDER

REGULAR BUILDER	SYSTEM BUILDER
Works in the business	Works on business
Depends on the system	Builds the system
Lives in a built house	Builds a house to live in
Waits for BPM	Everyday is a BPM day
Waits for upline	Wait for nobody
Builds step-by-step	Stumbles forward
Small picture/small dream	Big picture/big dream
Tries-to-learn attitude	Start-up-a-company attitude
Takes 3 years to understand the business	Takes 3 months to understand the business
Weak, reserved, negative most the time	Strong, excited, positive all the time
Slow decision-maker	Quick decision-maker
Uncoachable	Coachable
Doesn't see herself opening an office	Dying to open her own office

BUILDABLE PRODUCT

"Keep it simple. Keep it duplicatable."

Imagine if McDonald's sold gourmet food like steak and lobster. They would have to change the kitchens of all the McDonald's all over the world. They would have to retrain all their workers on how to cook a steak rare, medium rare, medium well, and well done. The complexity could cause the whole system to collapse.

Steak and seafood are not buildable products for McDonald's. But hamburgers and fries are. I'm not an expert in the kitchen, but I'm guessing their kitchens can't cook many different kinds of dishes. Plus they probably don't want to. They want to keep things simple. The simplicity of their system allows them to duplicate and multiply.

> These system builders know what products their business can build on, what's buildable and what's non-buildable.

McDonald's keeps it simple. They sell hamburgers, fries, and soft drinks. Starbucks too. Coffee is their thing. Jamba Juice just does juice. KFC focuses on chicken.

The hamburger is the buildable product of McDonald's. Coffee is the buildable product of Starbucks. Chicken is the buildable product of KFC. Juice is the buildable product of Jamba Juice.

McDonald's doesn't mind if their customers go to Jamba Juice for better drinks. They also don't mind if customers think their chicken nuggets can't compete with KFC's breasts and thighs.

"Focus on your core business.
There is enough business for everybody."

It is unbelievable to see that there are people in the building and duplication business who can't keep it simple.

It is amazing how complicated some people are becoming, as if they're trying to do everything for everybody. They learn everything, compare everything, but recruit nobody and sell nothing.

Even if they recruit someone, their recruit will be dead on arrival. They scare the new recruit with all the products they hype up. These people always get excited about something new. They bring in all kinds of vendors and wholesalers to their office. This week Mr. A of company A says their product is the best, so the team gets excited. Next week, Mr. B of company B shows them their product is actually better, so the team gets more excited. The week after that, they bring in Mr. C, who claims that their product has even more benefits. Then next week, they talk about health insurance, then Property & Casualty, then mortgages.

> **Everybody's always excited. They go out and get all kinds of licenses, gather all kinds of materials— brochures, prospectuses, software—and get together with other teammates to study the new products and services.**

They go out to see clients and unload all the things they learned, all the products they offer. Then when they can't make money, they bring in the self-help guru. They go to seminars and get excited again. They go to another guru who teaches them how to sell. They go out to buy books on how to be a winner, a leader, a super salesperson, and a visionary.

When all these things don't work, they go to see the fortune teller or the feng shui master to learn how to align the office furniture and move the decorations in harmony with the cosmos, so that they can change their destiny. When they go home, they have problems with their spouse, so they sign up for marriage counseling.

CAN YOU FOCUS ON ONE THING AT A TIME?

Can you make one thing work first before jumping into another deal? If you try to master everything, you master nothing. Worse, your team can't duplicate you. And if they don't think they can do it, they won't stay. The "jack of all trades" won't be big and can't duplicate anybody.

Also, if you flip flop on too many things, your team won't know what you truly believe in. You must be consistent with your message and your actions.

Some people get very excited when the market is up but become so down when the market goes down. Do you still remember when you preached the virtues of dollar cost averaging and asset allocation? If you truly believe in our mission, you must be consistent. You can't sell something one day when it's hot and go sell other things when it's not so hot.

"Focus on your mission and persist in your actions."

BUILDING LONG DISTANCE

Why should you build long distance? There are millions of people around you. You can work your lifetime in your local area and never run out of recruits or sales. But there will be times when you need to go the distance.

1. IT'S THE PEOPLE, NOT THE LOCATION

Sometimes you can't find the right people in your local area because the superstars are out of town. In fact, you never know where your biggest builders live. This happened to me and many other builders too.

"It's not the size of the city.
It's the size of the leader that counts."

2. YOU HAVE TIME AND YOUR TEAM IS NOT THAT BUSY

Most of the time, you're not always that busy. You can squeeze out 1 or 2 days out of the week. In addition, most of your team has plenty of time. Why not be more efficient?

3. YOU AND YOUR TEAM MUST GET OUT OF YOUR COMFORT ZONES

Building long distance forces you to work harder. It forces you to do more BPMs, training, and business interviews. It's tough, but you grow faster.

4. GREATER VISION

Building long distance stretches your vision. You think bigger.

5. BETTER STRATEGY

When you build long distance, you are more strategic

in your actions, planning and preparing before acting, because you don't want to waste precious time.

6. YOU GET THE PING PONG EFFECT

Building long-distance will lead to more referrals and cross-recruiting from different locations. It will multiply your growth.

For example: Assume there is a new airline carrier.

1. The airline starts to fly between two cities: San Jose and Los Angeles.

SJ ⇨ LA

LA ⇨ SJ

SJ ⟷ LA

2 cities = 2 ways

2. The airline adds Houston to their schedule.

SJ ⇨ LA   LA ⇨ SJ

SJ ⇨ HS   HS ⇨ SJ

LA ⇨ HS   HS ⇨ LA

3 cities = 6 ways

3. The airline adds New York.

SJ ⇨ LA	SJ ⇨ NY	HS ⇨ LA
LA ⇨ SJ	NY ⇨ SJ	LA ⇨ HS
SJ ⇨ HS	LA ⇨ NY	NY ⇨ HS
HS ⇨ SJ	NY ⇨ LA	HS ⇨ NY

4 cities = 12 ways

It's easier to have geometric growth by building long distance because the ping pong effect creates multiplication.

THE NATURE OF A LONG DISTANCE TEAM

*"There are great
advantages to working with
people at a distance."*

1. THEY APPRECIATE YOU MORE. You make an effort to see your long-distance team, while your local people see you everyday and take you for granted.

2. THEY'RE MORE EAGER TO LEARN. They're hungry for information and training. They never seem to get enough.

3. THEY'RE MORE COACHABLE. Of course, they have to be, or else you may not come back.

4. THEY'RE MORE INDEPENDENT. They have no choice. They have no one to depend on. They do more work by themselves.

5. THEY DON'T COMPLAIN. If they do, you're not around to hear it anyway.

6. THEY ACCEPT REALITY. They experience the difficulty of the business sooner than if you held them by the hand since the day they joined.

7. THEY ALWAYS ASK YOU TO COME. They need you more than you need them.

8. THEY'RE WILLING TO PERFORM. They entice you with results for you to come back.

9. THEY'RE WILLING TO TRAVEL LIKE YOU. In the future, they tend to build long distance like you.

10. YOUR LOCAL TEAM BEGINS TO APPRECIATE YOU MORE AND NEEDS YOU MORE. As they say, "You don't know what you got till it's gone."

11. YOUR LOCAL TEAM BECOMES MORE INDEPENDENT. They now realize they can't rely on you all the time.

12. YOU CREATE MORE COMPETITION. More good news comes from different locations.

REFERRAL PROGRAM

If you're not ready to build long distance, or the new recruit at a distance is not ready, don't do it.

Instead you should refer your prospect to a local MD to take care of them and work out a solution for the benefit of all parties involved.

THE CHALLENGES OF BUILDING LONG DISTANCE

1. ARE YOU BUILDING THE RIGHT PEOPLE?

You must find out if they're the right people, if they want it bad enough.

PUT THEM ON THE SCALE. WHO WANTS IT MORE?

If they want you more than you want them, you win. If you want them more than they want you, you lose.

If they want to win more than you want them to win, you win. If you want them to win more than they want to win, you lose.

2. IS YOUR LOCAL TEAM LOSING?

If your local team is not strong enough, they may fall apart. Travel only if you know that it won't affect the local base much.

Thus, don't leave your base too long. In the early days, only travel 1 or 2 days a week and increase it later on when you see fit.

3. COST

Building long distance is a big investment of time and money. Make sure you can afford it. Make sure you're serious. Sooner or later, you will do it. It's just a matter of time.

> **REMEMBER:**
> • If you gain 5 people long distance and lose 10 people at home, you lose.
> • If you gain 10K long distance and lose 15K at home, you lose.

BUILD PEOPLE

Imagine building a house and having all the building blocks and beams, but forgetting the cement, the glue, and the nails to bind them together.

"Build with your heart. The cement puts all the building blocks together."

You may have early success. You may have large numbers of recruits, lots of sales, and impressive titles. You may dazzle people with your big house, your fancy car, and your expensive toys. But if you don't understand about building people, you won't make it in the business over the long haul.

> **YOUR PEOPLE ALWAYS WANT TO KNOW:**
> - your trustworthiness
> - your commitment
> - your capability
> - how much you care about them

BUILD YOURSELF FIRST

Before you can build people, you must build yourself first. It's a two way street between you and your teammate. What do you bring to the table?

BUILD RELATIONSHIPS

Know your people. Know their family. Know what they want, what's important to them.

Organize time to get together, so you can meet their spouse and their children. You may find out more about your teammates by talking to their spouse. If your spouse is involved, he or she can help you build rapport with your teammates' spouses.

They must feel that they're important to you. They're not just a code number.

> *"People quit a business,*
> *but they won't quit a friend."*

BUILD TRUST

Can your people trust you? Do you say what you mean and mean what you say?

What's your reputation? Can you improve it? Are you often late to meetings? Do you forget about appointments? Do you recognize your problems or do you just ignore them?

When you promise people something, would you deliver if challenges arise or if you have to take a loss? In a conflicting situation between you and your people, who wins?

> If it's 50/50: They win.
>
> If it's 60/40: They win.
>
> If it's 70/30: They win.
>
> If it's 80/20: They win.
>
> If it's 90/10: You win.

Only in a case where the evidence shows that you are 90% right and they are only 10% right, then the ruling will be in your favor.

For example: If you and your downline both know a guy, and you both approach him, and you are not sure who talked to him first, then the recruit should belong to your downline.

If you talk to the guy first, but he wants to think about it, and 10 days later on, your downline invites him to your BPM, and he joins, then he should join your downline.

If you invite the guy to a BPM, when he comes in and meets his best friend, who happens to be your downline, and he wants to join your downline instead of you, then your downline wins.

But if you fly to New York to recruit the guy, and when he joins you, your downline tells you that your new recruit is his best friend, then in this case, you can tell him to back off.

"You can't win on your people.
If you win on your people, you may end up losing.
If you lose on your people, you may end up winning.
When your people win, you will win."

BE A SERVANT LEADER

Put your people first. Put yourself last. Take care of them. Always do it first. Do it many times before you ask them to do it.

Stand up and stand by your people, especially through tough times. People may come and go. They may not appreciate you. But you always wait for them. They leave you. But you never leave them.

Always be proud of your people and be proud of your team. Everybody will be somebody, and everyone will win.

"Your commitment to the business and your people are the key. People won't commit until you commit."

LOOK FOR THE GOOD THINGS

Everyone is different. Everyone has their own strengths and weaknesses. Everyone has good qualities and bad qualities.

Focus on their strengths and their goodness. Like a teacher, be aware of your students' weaknesses but always focus on their strengths. Praise them and help them win.

BELIEVE IN YOUR PEOPLE

People have tough times in the business. Your belief in them is very critical.

Do you believe in the power of believing? When was the last time anybody really believed in you? Sometimes even your family doesn't believe in you. How great does it feel when someone sincerely believes in people like you and me?

Be the one who believes in your people. I do believe the greatest gift you can give to your people is to give them your total belief that they will be successful.

MAKE THEM FEEL GOOD

Make people feel good about themselves. Everyone is important to you and to the team, whether they're the big shot or the new person.

Give praise and recognition on everything they do, even on small achievements. Remember when you were small?

Lift them up. Share their successes to everybody. When they feel good, they do good.

Be for real when you deal with people. Don't be "plastic fantastic", saying things you don't really mean. Yes, we need to be upbeat and excited, but let's not be phoney. Otherwise, all the building effort has no substance.

BUILD CONFIDENCE

Most importantly, you've got to build confidence. If you are confident about your capability, your business know-how, your team will also gain more confidence, knowing that they follow someone who knows what he is doing.

You must master the business. Of course, there are things that you don't know. Be sincere. Don't "wing" it. If your team asks for things that you are not clear or sure about, tell them you will find out and will get back to them.

You must be committed to your goal. The team needs to know what you want to achieve. Imagine a passenger gets on a ship and the captain doesn't know how to operate it and doesn't know for sure where the destination is.

> **You build yourself to build people. The more people you build, the more you build yourself.**

IN THE PEOPLE BUSINESS:

- You do everything but expect nothing.

- You do it first. They do it later.

- You come first. They come last.
  They leave first. You leave last.

- You should never win over your people.

- If you say ten good things and one bad thing,
  they remember only the bad thing.

- They can criticize you. You can't
  criticize them.

- They come and go, but you always stay.

- They do and they don't, but you always do it.

- They may win or they may lose,
  but you have to win.

- You need them, but you don't need them.
  You care for them, but you don't care for them.

HAVE A HIGH LEVEL
OF TOLERANCE

"People are like the weather.
They change often."

In a highly competitive world, when we want to win so bad, it's easy for us to lose patience. We lose patience with ourselves, and we lose patience with our people.

ALWAYS GIVE THE BENEFIT OF THE DOUBT

Whenever people don't join or buy from you, or say something negative, be patient. They might've had a bad experience before. They might have personal problems. Maybe they've just undergone a crisis. Or maybe you talked to them at the wrong time on the wrong day. Don't get mad. Don't get even. Be tolerant.

When you go to the meeting and the speaker or the upline says something unpleasant, you may think they're pointing the finger at you. Give them the benefit of the doubt. Most of the time, they're probably talking about somebody else, and even if it is you, they're probably just trying to help. It could be that the way they express things are not well delivered.

When your people don't show up, when they fail to do something, when they drive you nuts, be patient. They probably don't mean it.

When the paperwork is screwed up, when the commissions are incorrect, when applications are returned, be patient. It could be their mistake, or it could be yours. When things have to change, be patient. There are probably good reasons. Always give people the benefit of the doubt. Always accept people's mistakes.

"To err is human, to forgive divine."

DON'T TAKE IT PERSONAL

When bad things can happen, they will happen. Murphy's law rules. Most of the time, problems aren't aimed at you. Don't take it personal. Don't hold grudges.

YOU'RE A LEADER

You must have big shoulders. You must have the ability to absorb adversity. You must show that you're bigger than the small things. You can forgive and forget. You focus on the big task.

PEOPLE CHANGE

Most people change. They'll be better to you. They'll appreciate you. They'll understand you. If you don't hold grudges, and if you don't close the door on them, they'll join you, buy from you, and follow you.

LEARN TO LIVE WITH PEOPLE

Don't ask for separation. When disputes occur, work it out. When arguments arise, listen to one another. If both persons are right, then who is wrong?

If you don't have perfect downlines, live with them.
If you don't have the best uplines, live with them.

When you win, you won't remember these things
anyway. When you get to the top of the mountain,
you won't worry about all the tough stuff. Your
people need to grow. You must have a high level
of tolerance to accept their mistakes.

"Give your downline a chance.
Give your upline a chance.
Give everyone a chance."

BUILDING GIANTS

*"You must build giants for
long term profitability and security."*

MD is the starting position. Some of them will develop to become giants, CEO MDs and above.

* A giant is a system builder with a strong organization.

* A giant has ambitious vision and passion for the mission. They stand out by their conviction and project a successful image of their future.

* A giant maintains a strong baseshop and builds strong frontline leaders. Thus he has a big super base through 1st.

* A giant overlaps leadership and builds a great superteam through 6 generations. A giant is generation blind and hierarchy blind, a pure builder.

* A giant has a great recruiting mentality and a builder's mindset, and maintains a strong recruiting and building machine throughout his organization.

* A giant masters the meeting and events.

* A giant is consistent and predictable.

* A giant is a proactive, positive team player.

* A giant has a good reputation.

* A giant, like a general, needs to be built up with responsibility and challenges.

* A giant can build and push up new giants.

Once a giant emerges, he can build, lead and duplicate MDs and builders. He can take charge and take care of his superteam. He can also grow them.

"Giants are our ultimate system builders."

MEETINGS & EVENTS

It's not about the meeting.

It's about the people

who go to the meeting.

It's not about the teacher.

It's about the student.

It's not about the speaker.

It's about the listener.

And it's not about the convention.

It's about the convention's goals

that determine

the success of the meeting.

But how successful it is depends on you.

BUILD PEOPLE FROM EVENT TO EVENT

FROM SMALL MEETING TO BIG MEETING:

HOME MEETING

* Build relationships
* Get to know the family

HOME BMP / BPM

* Recruit and invite
* Lead by example
* Foster duplication
* Create passion for the mission
* Sell the dream to potential new prospects

OFFICE BPM

* Sell the dream to the team
* Recruit new people

> You can tell whether a person is serious about the business by watching him/her go to the BPM. Most people who show up Tuesday nights won't show up Saturday mornings. And unfortunately most people who show up Saturday mornings won't show up Tuesday nights. You can hardly find anybody who can go to both BPMs consistently. If you have one, you have a potential builder.

Meeting after the Meeting - MD Club
+ Manage team activities
+ Be accountable for results

Upstart School
+ Build a believer in the business

MD Club
+ Monitor and build new MDs
+ Learn to recruit and duplicate

MD School
+ Build future big basehop builders

Execlub
+ Build future big hierarchy builders
+ Build a MD Factory

Annual Convention
+ Stretch vision
+ Bring the team to a higher level
+ Fulfill major commitments
+ Make major decisions
+ Provide giant food for giants

"You can't build people's minds.
Big events can."

DON'T TRY TO CHANGE PEOPLE

During my career, I saw so many leaders trying to change people. Most of them sincerely believed that their job was to change people for the better.

AS A RESULT, MOST LEADERS TRIED EVERYTHING:

- More meetings
- More training
- More contests
- More motivation
- More counseling
- More coaching

THESE EFFORTS HAVE SOME INFLUENCE, BUT ONLY A LITTLE, MAYBE 10%

"I believe 90% of change comes from inside the person, from a personal decision to change."

IF YOU CANNOT CHANGE YOUR PEOPLE, THEN CHANGE YOUR PEOPLE

The only thing you can do is to recruit more people into your organization and the ones who want to win will emerge.

Most people won't change. Most people resist change. Most people won't change fast enough or significantly enough to help them win. That's why most people won't make it.

Don't try to change people. It will only create agony and frustration for you. Just accept people the way they are.

WHY IT IS NEARLY IMPOSSIBLE TO CHANGE YOUR PEOPLE

You're not a prophet in your own land. Your people will not listen to you, and if they do, they won't listen seriously. But when they go to the big event, they listen to other people.

Most people do not like to be told to change. They will change only from a personal decision deep inside of them and from somebody or something said that they can relate to.

"You cannot change people, but you can bring people to life-changing events.
You cannot build people, but you can bring people to big building events."

GREAT EVENTS:
THE CHANGING MACHINE

*"You can never build a big team unless
you understand the importance of the big event."*

◆ In a big event, there is magic in crowds. The environment creates a condition for change.

◆ When people travel far away from home and spend money and time, they listen more seriously.

◆ When people travel, the team works together with more intensity and urgency.

**Small minds
worship big people.**

**Average minds
worship big things.**

**Great minds
worship big events.**

◆ People tend to compare themselves with others. When they see someone just like them do it, they think, "If he can do it and if she can do it, I can do it too."

*"There are people who tell us there are
too many meetings.
I think that's wonderful. The way I see it,
there should be too many meetings
so that we have too many chances
to change people's lives.*

THE MEETING BEFORE THE MEETING, THE MEETING AFTER THE MEETING

Just as the appetizer and the dessert could be as important as the main dish, the meeting before the meeting and the meeting after the meeting could be as important as the meeting itself.

CREATE A MEETING MENTALITY

As a great general with a great army never goes into battle without preparation, a great leader with a great team never goes into an event without a meeting before the meeting.

Great system builders pay special attention to the meetings before and after the BPM, the BMP, and the big event.

The meeting after the meeting is the secret of a dominant team. Start strong, finish strong, and take the next step after an event.

Most successful builders meet before the BPM to prepare for the operation and meet after the BPM to cap-

> ◆ When taking teams to big events, the preparation, the briefing, and the mindset before entering the event ensures success during the event.
>
> ◆ The meeting after the event is also very critical because commitments and decisions will be made to elevate the team to the next level.

ture and evaluate the results of their activities, just like most business owners who always come early to prepare for opening and always stay late to review the results of the day before closing.

DON'T GET KILLED BY THE MEETING

Meetings are good. Meetings are our business. But too many meetings can hurt us.

I remember during my social worker career, it all started with some meetings and some committees. But over time, I found myself going to meetings all day, all week long. Meetings at the city level, meetings at the county level, meetings at the state level, meetings at the federal level, meetings with different agencies, meetings with non-profit organizations, meetings with the neighborhood community, meetings with the business community, and meetings to bring all this information back to our staff.

I realized one day that the time we spend to service our clients is so little. Worse, by the time we get to our clients, it's usually too little, too late, and we're too exhausted.

"Meetings create more meetings, good or bad!"

There are many offices where the MDs and the leaders get bogged down with too many meetings and too much paperwork—meetings for the office, the task force, compliance, conference calls, etc.

> REMEMBER: This is a business. You need to make money. And your people need to make money.
> Maximize meetings: Spend 90% of your time on activities with recruits and clients or anything related to recruits and sales.
> Minimize meetings: Spend 10% of your time on activities related to paperwork and procedures or anything not related to recruits and sales.

BUILDING ON EXCITEMENT, BUILDING ON INSPIRATION

We have a lot of excitement, promotions and contests. When business is slow and we want to crank up results, we tend to resort to some contest, trip, award, or promotion run, or we invite a motivational speaker to speak to our team.

Oftentimes it may not be enough or provide lasting results. We need to look deep inside to see what truly inspires people.

EXCITEMENT	INSPIRATION
Recruit	Build
Make a sale	Help a family
Make money	Make a difference
Run for the title	Grow the team to the next level
Powerful speaker	Example of success
Outside	Inside
Short term	Long term

We need people to be excited. But if people are inspired, it is more genuine and long lasting. It's hard to have an outside speaker motivate while local leaders are not going out to the field and leading by example.

"Focus on inspiration, not motivation."

THE DYNAMICS OF A MEETING

We don't run the meeting. We create the meeting. We are one of the most dynamic forces in the financial services industry. Our meetings change all the time. Although we have a planning committee, we really just have a general feeling of what we want to do. So I know we're going to drive those guys in the industry crazy. But that's the way it is. There's a totally different animal sitting here. Even me, I don't know what I'm going to do in the meeting. But that ensures we have the best meeting.

THE MISSION
&
THE CRUSADE

The joy of life can't be

just good food, nice clothes, fancy cars,

and a happy family.

It includes the pain of defeat,

the hurt of endurance,

the fear of trying, the giving,

and the sacrifice for a cause

that benefits others.

SELLING UNDERSTANDING VS SELLING THE PRODUCT

In the financial industry, there are many products and many salespeople. Some spend all their lives selling term insurance. Some work for companies that sell only whole life. Some just sell VUL. Some specialize in nothing but annuities.

Many people jump into selling investment products when the stock market is hot, while others sell mortgage when interest rates are low.

Companies spend a fortune to develop new products, hire new salespeople, and advertise to make products more appealing. Yet people are still in a world of hurt. Lack of savings, mounting debt, and rising bankruptcy are the norms of today. Very few people are willing to sit down on a regular basis to make people understand important concepts, how money works, their financial picture, and priorities of their future.

Some buy a variety of insurance products but lack savings and investments. Some have different kinds of savings and

> When buying computers, many people buy hardware not knowing whether it suits their computing needs. But if they understand their software needs, they can buy the right hardware that will be up to the job.
>
> If you're buying a home sound system, a receiver, speakers, DVD and mixer, without understanding their power or compatibility, when you hook it up, it may not work.

investments without understanding the need for protection. Some get a new mortgage but may create more debt and more spending.

Quite often the person who sells insurance, investments, real estate or mortgage hardly pays attention to other important aspects of their clients' financial needs. They also tend to see clients once and never come back to check up on them again.

> You cannot see a doctor once and expect to stay healthy. The same is true with your car, which needs regular maintenance. Likewise your financial situation needs to be assessed on a regular basis.

It's not the product but the financial understanding that's more important. If people understand their needs, then they can buy the products that suit their needs.

VISION OF A NEW INDUSTRY

This is the financial industry but it's not. We just happen to be one of the best marketing, the most powerful, the most magnificent distribution systems in the world. Why do we want to be in this industry? This is one of the largest, most powerful, most important industries in the world.

THE OLD INDUSTRY	THE NEW INDUSTRY
Focus on sale	Focus on concept
Focus on product	Focus on solution
Focus on features & benefits	Focus on need & affordability
Focus on closing	Focus on understanding
Present the sale	Share information
One time deal	Regular checkup
Singular need	Overall picture
Customer	Client
Usually have quotas	No quotas
Commission	Mission
Recruit salespeople	Open outlets
Sell locally	Build and expand

HOW TO MAKE A SALE

"It's not about making a sale.

It's all about how you feel about what you do."

After a decade of going out in the field, I learned that unless I feel good about myself and about what I do, and unless I feel good about the company and the product I represent, everything else is useless.

> **THE FOUR ELEMENTS OF MAKING A SALE:**
> - **Feel Good about Yourself**
> - **Feel Good about Your Company and Your Product**
> - **Give a Simple Presentation**
> - **Let Them Make the Decision**

FEEL GOOD ABOUT YOURSELF, FEEL GOOD ABOUT YOUR COMPANY, FEEL GOOD ABOUT YOUR PRODUCT

I share the challenges of many people. When I started the business, most of the people around me, my friends and my family, did not believe in me. That attacked my confidence, and I didn't feel too good about what I did.

In the early days, when I went out and made some money, I felt I did a good job. But deep down there was something that held me back.

Whenever I went to a party, and people asked me what I do, I'd always say I'm in financial services, although at the time I sold life insurance. And when they asked me what kind of insurance I sell, I didn't even want to tell them. It took me a long time to say I sell life insurance.

In fact, many times I just wished that I failed. There was a part of me that thought it would just be easier to take a No than go on. I hoped that when I got to the people's homes, they would tell me, "I'm busy. I can't see you."

I would feel so good if they told me that. "I can go home now," I'd say to myself. "They're busy. It's not my fault." No wonder many people didn't buy from me.

But once in a while, when I felt strongly about what I did, when I was fired up after attending a great meeting, people bought from me and joined me.

And the more I went out in the field, the more I realized that the things that held me back had nothing to do with the product or the marketplace. Rather, I was worrying too much about what other people thought about me.

> I woke up to the fact that I don't just make a sale. I change people's lives. I help people take care of their families. I vowed to myself never to sell to people unless I felt strongly about my contribution.

From then on I went out in the field with pride. I knew that I was going to affect every family I talked to. Selling became less painful and less fearful. In fact, I began to like it. Now, I love to talk to people. I love to share with them what I know. That has made all the difference.

GIVE A SIMPLE PRESENTATION

Keep it simple. Don't overload people with facts and figures. It's important that people understand the financial concepts and what our services and products can do for them. Make sure people understand the benefits as well as the costs. Make sure it's good for them.

> **REMEMBER:** Most clients do not have the sophisticated knowledge that you have. How much you know does not matter. What matters is how much they understand.

TIME YOURSELF. People don't have the whole night to listen.

LET THEM MAKE THE DECISION

> *"The real secret to making a sale:*
> *There is no secret."*

A few years into the business, one night, all of a sudden, I got enlightened. I figured out the secret of closing a sale.

PEOPLE MAKE UP THEIR OWN MINDS

* Those people who want to buy–they will buy.

* Those people who don't want to buy–no matter what–they won't buy.

After that realization, every night when I went out in the field and talked to people, I knew whether or not a client wanted to buy. My sixth sense told me that the person who wants to buy will give me a check and the person who doesn't won't.

So if you want to have a great closing ratio, sell only to the person who wants to buy. And if the person doesn't want to buy, don't sell to him.

"You don't make a sale. You share important information that may help change people's lives."

SELLING: DIFFICULT OR EASY?
"It's up to you."

To most people, selling is probably one of the most difficult things in the world. That's how I felt early on. But as time passed, I found out it's not as hard as I thought.

1. PEOPLE ARE DIFFERENT

Some people are difficult, some people are easy, and some people who seem to be difficult at first actually turn out to be not that difficult at all.

2. I CAN'T SELL

Most of us think that you have to be a slick salesperson for people to buy. Nothing is further from the truth. Actually most clients like to see the sincere belief and conviction in you.

You will be surprised by the number of people who will buy from you. During my first few years, I always wondered why people bought from me despite the fact that my presentation skills were not so good.

3. You Have No Quotas

You're in business for yourself. Nobody forces you to sell. You have no quotas. You have no pressure. Most of the time, you're part-time, you have a job, and you have other sources of income. Whether or not you make a sale, it won't make or break you.

4. It's Not a Job

It's not a job. You're not an employee of a sales force. You do this because you like it. You want to do it. You love going out in the field and helping people. So if you love what you do, and if you believe in what you do, it's not that difficult, is it?

5. You Look for the Believers

Most of the time, while sharing the concepts and products, you don't just make a sale. Your potential client could be a potential recruit who believes in what we do and may join us to go out and share our mission.

6. It's a Numbers Business

Ultimately, it's a numbers business. There are good days. There are bad days. If you see more people, you have more chances. In this world, when someone is selling something, somebody is buying something.

7. It Only Seems Difficult at First

After your first 3 or 4 sales, you will begin to feel good. After 15 to 20 sales, you will feel great. After 30 to 40 sales, you are in business. Just like anything in life, success breeds more success.

NEVER TRY TO BE A SALESPERSON

I'm not sure this is the right approach or the right thinking, but in the last 19 years of being in the "sales business," I never thought of myself as a salesperson nor wanted to be so good in sales.

I have nothing against selling, a sales career, or salespeople. In fact, I'm quite good at making the sale. I made good money most of my career through personal sales, training sales, and referral sales.

I also believe that if you're not a good personal producer, it will be hard for you to become a good trainer, and, therefore, it will be more difficult for you to be a big basehop and hierarchy builder.

However, I have a strong belief that if you have a good product and you bring real value to the client, you don't need to be a good salesperson. Recruiting, too. If you have a for real opportunity, you don't need to be a good recruiter.

"You just sell to the person who wants to buy and recruit the person who wants to join."

A System Builder Will Bring out Better Results and More Sales than a Salesperson

Normal salespeople sell products. System builders sell the system, opening the outlets that will move products on a much bigger scale.

I like to make a sale. But I love to do training sales. During training sales, I get to make the sale as well as train the future trainers of my organization. I also don't want to be too good, too "professional", or too slick in sales, because my people cannot duplicate it. I'd rather make a simple sale that can be duplicated rather than make a sophisticated, non-duplicatable sale.

"Salespeople pay attention to the close of the sale.

Builders pay attention to the mission,

the crusade of the sale, and the learning of the

trainee during the sales process. "

Thus, if you make a complicated sale, a nagging sale or a lengthy sale, even if you get the sale, you lose the trainee.

Sometimes, the best sale you make is the sale you don't make. Have the courage and will to walk out of a difficult or inappropriate situation. Even if you do not make the sale, you may actually make the best impression to your trainee/teammate.

SELLING TO YOUR DOWNLINE

"The most important sale is
the sale to your recruit or your downline."

Your downline must know the reason why they buy, not because they're your downline and not because they joined.

They buy because they recognize how good the products are for their family and for their needs. They must understand the concept and know their financial situation and their goal. They believe in our mission. They see what we do to help people. They see our crusade.

They must see the benefits, feel great about the sale process, and be proud about the transaction.

The secret of your success is not because you're a good salesperson. It's because you do it right. You do it with pride. Your recruit/downline will remember their first sale experience for the rest of their lives.

"We don't want a sale. We want an inspiration."

YOUR CLIENTS ARE MORE THAN JUST A SALE

"Build a large base of multi-product using clients."

1. KEEP A LIST OF ALL YOUR CLIENTS

Not only do you need a large base of recruits. You need to retain a large base of clients who may want and need multiple products.

2. CALL AND VISIT YOUR CLIENTS AND ASK FOR MORE REFERRALS

Satisfied clients give the best referrals. Your clients will have new friends and acquaintances whom they could refer you to.

3. CLIENTS NEED REGULAR FINANCIAL HEALTH CHECK UPS

Your clients appreciate it when you check in from time to time. They may need some adjustment or additional coverage to their policy. They may need to start a college fund for their new child or find out about more ways to invest their money.

4. RECRUIT YOUR CLIENTS

Timing is everything. The client who wasn't interested a year ago might be interested today. Most clients or their spouses do have some degree of interest in our business. At the very least, they already are convinced about the products and concepts. All you have to do is talk about the opportunity. It is just a matter of time.

WHY PEOPLE DON'T BUY

TWO MAIN REASONS:

1. They don't understand the concept/product.

2. They don't believe or trust you.

When people don't understand, they will not make a decision. Make sure to ask them if there is anything they do not understand. Also, people don't buy because either they don't believe you or they don't trust you.

♦ Be sincere. Tell it like it is. Show them the advantages as well as the disadvantages.

♦ If you can afford not to make a sale, you can make a sale. The times when you want to make a sale so bad are the times when you can't make a sale.

THE HIDDEN REASONS

Many times, when I thought I had an obvious sale, I could never close. This drove me crazy. Later on, I found out that there were so many hidden reasons. The clients' marriage was in chaos. They're in financial trouble. One of them has serious health problems. And many other reasons. But of course, they wouldn't disclose that information to me.

> Imagine you own a clothing store, and someone walks in, looks interested in a shirt, and tries it on, but doesn't buy it. Don't knock your head against the wall trying to figure out why the person didn't buy.

This realization reduced my frustration and saved my career. I thought that there was something wrong with me or something wrong with my presentation. Maybe it was the way I talked, or maybe I was not excited enough.

Now, the way I see it, if they don't buy, they don't buy. All I can do is give them my best. It's their life. It's their decision.

When a friend or relative doesn't buy, many of us tend to take it personally. Relax. They'll buy someday. And even if they don't, your career cannot rely solely on a handful of friends or relatives anyway. If you're a real estate broker and bank your career on your circle of friends and relatives, your career won't last too long. You don't open a restaurant on that basis either. It's business, my friend.

SELL ONLY TO THE PERSON WHO REALLY WANTS TO BUY

In my career there are always friends and relatives who say, "Since you're my relative/best friend, I will buy from you."

> **Please, don't do me any favors.**

This seems good, but it's not. I would tell them, "No, don't do me any favors. I want you to buy only if you need it and because it benefits your family, then I would appreciate you a lot more!"

"Easy come, easy go.
Most easy sales are easily canceled!"

- If they do you a favor, later on, when they meet other friends or relatives who sell similar things, they may cancel your policy and do the other friend or relative a favor. I've seen many clients change their policies or investments because a close friend or relative told them to.

- If they do you a favor and buy, in the long term, they won't feel good about it, even if they keep it. And of course, you will feel like you owe them, which is not good either.

- If they buy from you as a favor, they won't recommend you or the product to others. You may miss the opportunity to serve many other families.

We do people a favor by educating them. Our job is not to make a sale. Our purpose is to help people take charge of their financial future. Thus, when they decide to buy, they must know exactly what they're getting into.

This is not a shirt or a pair of shoes. This is a long-term commitment that requires a lot of discipline. If they don't understand the product and concepts, they won't keep the product long term. In the end, it serves no one if they cancel early.

We don't do anybody a service when people cancel. If we convince people to buy, and they cancel, they may lose money, and that's even worse than if they didn't buy. So please, don't do me a favor!

> REMEMBER:
> When selling to good friends or relatives, make sure both husband and wife listen and understand. Don't take any short cuts.
> The same holds true for recruiting. Don't recruit anyone who is only doing you a favor.

A NEW CONCEPT
IN THE COMPENSATION SYSTEM

*"I'd rather have 1% of 100 people's efforts
than 100% of my own effort."*

– J. PAUL GETTY

How do you explain the difference between a system based on sales and one based on building? Most of the industry out there normally doesn't recruit or build. We do. We focus on building a large network of outlets, a large number of team members who are licensed.

TRADITIONAL SALES VS SPREAD AND OVERRIDES

In the following illustrations, note that Mr. A, Mr. B, and everyone under Mr. B are fully licensed. The three examples are simply hypothetical scenarios intended to help illustrate the concept of spread. This is a conceptual description, not the actual spread of this company or any company, because it varies from one company to the other.

As you can see, in the first example, we split 100% into 80% and 20%. Thus, if Mr. B sells, he only makes 80%, but he recruits 5 people and builds them. So, if tonight Mr. A makes 1 sale, he would make 100%. But if Mr. B and his 5 people each make 1 sale, Mr. B would earn 180% in total—80% from his own sale and 100% from overrides of 20% of 5 people's sales.

In the 2nd example, if Mr. A makes 1 sale, he still

A Conceptual Explanation of Spread and Overrides

Sale: Focus on high personal contract

Building: Focus on many levels of override/spread

MR. A   # MR. B

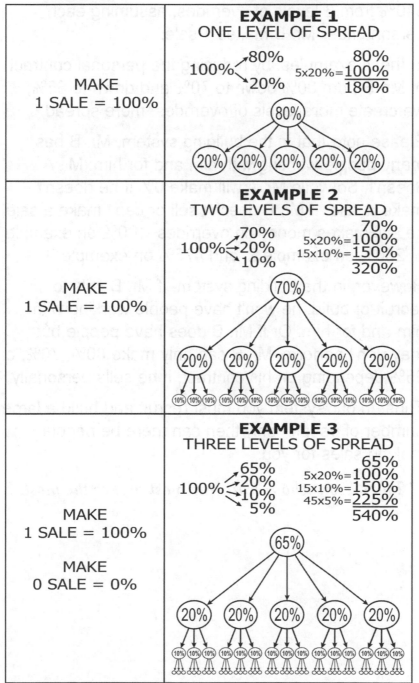

EXAMPLE 1
ONE LEVEL OF SPREAD

MAKE
1 SALE = 100%

100% →80%
      →20%

80%
5x20%=100%
      180%

EXAMPLE 2
TWO LEVELS OF SPREAD

MAKE
1 SALE = 100%

100% →70%
      →20%
      →10%

70%
5x20%=100%
15x10%=150%
      320%

EXAMPLE 3
THREE LEVELS OF SPREAD

MAKE
1 SALE = 100%

MAKE
0 SALE = 0%

100% →65%
      →20%
      →10%
      →5%

65%
5x20%=100%
15x10%=150%
45x5%=225%
      540%

earns 100%. But if Mr. B makes 1 sale, and each of his 1st and 2nd generation makes 1 sale, he overrides 2 levels now, totaling 320%. In the 3rd example, Mr. A still makes 100% from 1 sale, but Mr. B makes 540% from 3 levels of overrides, assuming each person under Mr. B makes 1 sale.

In these examples, by reducing the personal contract of Mr. B from 80% down to 70% and down to 65%, we create more levels of overrides, more spread.

Please note that in the building system, Mr. B has many people working with him and for him. Mr. A doesn't. So while Mr. A will make 0% if he doesn't make a sale, if Mr. B doesn't sell or can't make a sale, he still makes money on overrides—100% on example 1, 250% on example 2, and 475% on example 3.

However, in the building system, if Mr. B fails to recruit or build, he won't have people working with him and for him. Or if Mr. B does have people but they don't perform, Mr. B can only make 80%, 70%, or 65% depending on his contract, if he sells personally.

Thus, in our system you must recruit and build a large number of people, only then can there be people making sales for you.

"The person who recruits the most makes the most."

TEAM BUILDING

The Ladder of Evolution

From nobody to
UPSTART

From upstart to
CONTENDER

From contender to
WINNER

From winner to
CHAMPION

From champion to
DYNASTY

— P AT R ILEY

TEAMWORK MAKES THE DREAM WORK

"Team: Together Everyone Achieves More"

The purpose of a team is to win, and win bigger than any individual could. A team needs team players, and they must expect that they and their team will win.

Many people in the team building business want to build a team but can't be a team player themselves.

Here, we are in business for ourselves but not by ourselves.

> A fool is the person who trusts everyone but also the person who trusts no one.

BE PART OF THE TEAM: It's not I, me, mine. It's we, us, ours. Put the team first.

TRUST: When there is doubt about and lack of trust among members, there will be no team or the individual won't engage.

Give people a chance, give people the benefit of the doubt. Give your leader, your trainer, and your team a chance to work with you.

COMMIT TO A MISSION: Without a shared goal, we don't have a team. Our team is committed to the mission of making a difference for families.

FIGHT TO WIN: You work as an individual, but you fight as a team. Teamwork gives you more strength and courage to win. When the team wins, you also win.

BUILD THE TEAM: When you're in the team, so are your teammates. Together everyone can build a team naturally.

TEAM SPIRIT: In the team business, moody people are not very good for the team. Team members need to be positive, upbeat, and coachable. They need to stumble forward, lead by example, and persevere.

Helping others is also at the heart of being a team player. Thus, in our business, not only our teammates but also our clients benefit from this spirit.

Dreamwork: Through a large number of people who join hands for a common goal, everyone can win. Teamwork is dreamwork. It can make your dreams come true.

COMPETITION:
THE NATURE OF THE TEAM

"A team that does not compete is

a team that lacks purpose and unity."

In the team business, you need to recognize that the very nature of the team is to compete. Without competition, there is no game, no team to compete with.

You need to open up and work with others. An isolated team will be suffocated with boredom and have no momentum.

There are many people who think that this is a sales organization or a financial services business. "Why bother with competition and recognition?" they say. There are quite a few who are even more sarcastic: "Don't bother with the plaque. Just send me the check!"

You can be a loner with that attitude, but you won't make it in a team. You can't build a team without having your teammates compete with each other and with other teams.

You need to bring your team to the big event. The big event is like the Super Bowl, the ultimate arena of competition.

"Every time we compete or run for a goal,

a promotion, or a challenge,

the team rises up to a new level

and new stars are born."

Teams grow with competition. Competition builds and
tests leaders. You will find out how people perform
under pressure, how they play when they're hurt.

*"Your job as a coach and as a leader is
to talk about winning all the time."*

TEAM = PEOPLE + CARE

Anytime I see an office, a baseshop, or a hierarchy in bad shape, I look for the missing element: care.

Most of the time the cause of the problem lies among 10 reasons:

1. The leader cares less about his business.

2. The leader is distracted.

3. The leader begins to cool down.

4. The leader cares less about what's going on with the team.

5. The leader lacks communication.

6. The leader lacks overlapping leadership.

7. The leader cares little whether their team wins or not.

8. The team members are selfishly shielding.

9. The team members do not volunteer or respond to the upline's challenges.

10. Each leg in the team cannot work and cooperate together.

Like a sports team, if each player in the organization does not care for each other and does not care to win, you don't have a team.

A lot of people work for money, but that's not necessarily the most important thing to them. Rather, it's the team that they're working with and the leader that they follow that both play a big part of their performance.

Every night, there are many people in your
team who stay awake and think about you.
They probably ponder 3 things:
- Your Integrity
- Your Commitment
- If You Care About Them

*"People don't care about how much you know.
They just want to know how much you care."*

FOLLOW YOUR UPLINE, FOLLOW YOUR DOWNLINE, FOLLOW YOUR SIDELINE

"If the blind lead the blind,
both shall fall in the ditch."

– MATTHEW 15:14

Who should you follow? Should you follow your upline? Your upline has more experience, but what if your upline is on the wrong path? Should you follow your downline? Your downline is the source for potential recruits and production, but what if your downline is not moving? Should you follow your sideline? They're part of the office, but what if they have a different way of doing things?

"Follow your upline, and you may go up.
Follow your downline, and you may go down.
Follow your sideline, and you may
go around and around."

It's incredible how people slow down or get destroyed because of the people around them.

Students get poor grades or sidetracked. Employees get lost, confused and frustrated in their jobs. The same is true with people in this business. Instead of following success, pursuing their dream, submitting to the proven system, and aligning with successful builders, they tend to look around, find out more, and analyze every single issue. It doesn't take long to get them confused and frustrated before they lose their dream.

"Follow the truth, follow your heart,
follow your dream."

TOO LOYAL

*"Silence in the face of injustice makes
a coward out of man."*

I watched a movie recently about a family. The husband
is a really bad guy. He beats his wife, but every time he
abuses her, he comes up with lies to make up with her,
so she's happy again. Then he abuses
his child. The child tells her mother. He
denies everything, and she believes
him. Then he abuses the child again.
The child complains, and the mother
gets mad. He apologizes and says he
won't do it again. The story goes on.

> **It's not a movie.
> It's life. Most
> people are very
> loyal. Loyalty is a
> great virtue, but
> it can easily be
> abused.**

Throughout my life, I saw it all
around me. Many housewives all
over the world are loyal to their
husbands, many people are loyal to their family,
many subordinates are loyal to their boss—in spite of
frequent injustices done to them or to others.

It's the issue of integrity versus loyalty. Which one
comes first?

How loyal are you to your parents if they're wrong?
How loyal are you to your leader if he no longer
follows the successful path? What about the downline? What about your business?

Don't get me wrong. This is not meant to create any
conflict. I just don't want you to let the distracted
upline who is slowing down hurt your business. I want
you and your people to have the courage to stay on
track to your dreams.

THE SHIELDING EFFECT

"Cover the grass from sunshine, and it will die."

Shielding happens when an upline decides to shield his downline or his team from a higher upline.

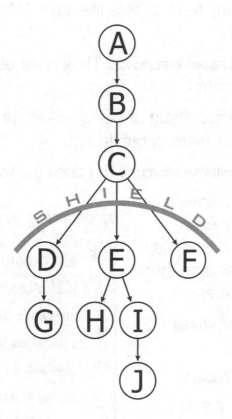

C is the "shielder". C shields his team from A and B.

D, E, F, G, H, I, J are the "shieldees".

There are so many reasons why people shield. Here are the most popular:

1. DOESN'T LIKE THE UPLINE: Somehow C doesn't get along or simply doesn't like B or A.

2. WAITS FOR LICENSE: Greed is the cause.

3. EGO: They may not want the team to be exposed to more knowledgeable, more powerful, and more successful leaders.

4. SELFISH: They treat people like toys. "My team belongs to me!"

5. AFRAID OF LOSING INFLUENCE: They want everyone under their control.

6. LAZY: They are afraid of being asked for bigger numbers or for more commitment.

7. HATES MEETINGS AND EVENTS: "If I don't go, you don't go."

8. INSECURE: Believe it or not, some are even afraid the downline may perform better than them and surpass them.

9. AND TONS OF OTHER REASONS...

So WHO'S TO BLAME?

The shielder, C? Yes, C's the one.

The shieldees, D, E, F, G, H, I, and J? Yes, they're the ones.

Why? Because they let C do it to them! They're

EXCEPTION: In some rare instances, when A and B are really the bad guys, it is justified for C to protect his team from negative influences. The problem is, who's to judge whether A and B are good or bad? What about C? Is C good or bad? Well, nobody really knows who's the bad guy, and nobody would admit that either, especially the bad guy!

independent businesspeople. Nobody can control them unless they let them. So please do not act like a victim if this ever happens to you.

Most often the end result of a shielding situation is a dead team or, at best, a struggling one.

"Shielding is a no-win situation!"

LEADER OR BUILDER

Leadership is everything. But in our business, leadership alone may not be enough. There is a misunderstanding about the role of a leader versus that of a builder.

In fact, many people prefer to be a leader rather than a builder. When they have people under them, they want to lead so bad that they forget they really need to be a builder first. They develop "leadership" skills like talking, teaching, and motivating instead of doing, field training, duplicating and showing results. They get so good, so slick, so high-level, so complicated that one day they're no longer duplicatable.

> **BUILDER'S TRAP:**
>
> After hitting the MD position, many people fall into this trap and a good number of higher ups slow down significantly on building.

There are areas in life that need leaders. But in a system where duplication is key, builders are needed. In building systems like Wal Mart, Starbuck's, McDonald's, or Home Depot, you don't really hear a lot about their leaders, but you know they have a lot of silent builders.

BUILDERS ARE NOT PROBLEM SOLVERS

In the people business, you deal with lots of people. Every one of them is different. They have different ideas, opinions, situations, challenges, and a lot of problems.

How to Deal with These Problems?

Don't. Except for a handful of serious issues related to the business that you must deal with, the large majority of people's problems are a waste of time.

> So many people would love to bring you their problems, as long as you're willing to take them.

If you stay in this business long enough, you'll be amazed by the amount of problems people have or create for themselves and then bring to you.

When people go to work at a job, they seem to mention no problems. Yet when people come into our business, they will have an endless list of problems: "I have no time... My car broke down... I have babysitting challenges... My spouse is not happy... I have other things to do first..."

They never say any of this to their boss. On the job, if you show up, they pay. If you don't show up, they won't pay, or they fire you. They don't need to know about your problems.

♦ **You can't solve family problems.** For most couples, the problems of their relationship normally existed before they joined the business.

◆ **YOU CAN'T LOAN PEOPLE MONEY.** First, you can never have enough money to loan to everybody. Second, you often just delay a bigger problem.

◆ **YOU CAN'T RECRUIT FOR THEM.** They have to prospect, go out, stay motivated, and do what is necessary to hit their goal.

◆ **YOU CAN'T SELL FOR THEM.** They have to go out in the field, get referrals, and learn to sell on their own initiative.

◆ **YOU CAN ASSIST.** You can support them up to a certain point. But you can't do their job.

◆ **People need to overcome their own problems.** They need to overcome their own challenges. They need to talk to and get support from their own families. They need to reorganize their life for their business, to do what's important for them and their families.

"You're not a problem solver!"

REMEMBER:

You're a leader. You're not
a marriage counselor.
You're not a psychiatrist.
You're not a banker.
You're not a social worker.
You're not a taxi driver.
You're not a babysitter.
You're a builder.

NEVER GIVE UP

The whole nature of our business is to do something we thought was impossible. That's why we get together to draw on each other's energy and unleash the giant power inside us.

I could not do what I did today had I not believed in myself and my people. I could never build a big team if I didn't believe deadly in every single one of you.

The reason I stick to people through thick and thin—even the worst guy, and I never leave them no matter what—is because I know they're going to win. I'm willing to go through nights and weeks, fly across the country, because I know they're going to win.

Hey guys, you cannot take shortcuts.

The reason you lose is because you give up too quickly on your people. But do you know what's the real reason? You give up on you. Most of you give up on you. It reflects from inside you to the outside. If you know you're going to win anyway, you never give up on anybody else.

You can't give up. It's sad when I see you give up on your people because that's when you give up on yourself.

I'm not trying to criticize anybody. There were times in my career when I slowed down too. I'm not a superman. There were times I wanted to give up on people too. There were times I wanted to give up on myself. I wanted to throw in the towel everyday. Everyday in the last 19 years I asked myself, "Should I slow down tomorrow?"

Quitting is not an option, but slowing down is always an option, which is equal to quitting for me. You don't have to completely quit. You just quit trying.

I only have one chance right now in my life, and the older I am the more I feel how precious my life is. Maybe I think in reverse, but I think about the time I live on this Earth. Life is too short. Click, you're thirty years old. Click, next thing you're forty. Click, you're fifty. And I hate the next click.

Please don't give up on yourself. And please believe in your people. And if you don't believe in yourself, why the heck are you here? You expect people to follow people like you, who always doubt yourself, always shaky?

If you don't believe in our people and our mission, why are you here? I think the guy who collects overrides and disappears at least has some integrity. At least he says to the whole world, "You know what? I just want the money." At least he declares his intentions publicly.

You cannot be a leader and tell people to follow you if you act like a wimp. You're killing people! You cannot allow yourself to be weak. When you take people to follow you, you have to be strong.

This is a fight. You don't have to have big numbers to say you're winning. You win when you have small numbers! You win best when you're down! I don't care if you do 5K or 10K in your base. But you act like a winner! You act like a leader! Then, you lead people.

The smaller numbers you have, the stronger you should be to your team. The bigger the trap you're in, the stronger you should be to your team, because at the worst of times your people look up to you. Imagine you're captain of a ship and when you get lost, you don't know what to do. It's the worst of times. That's why we need you.

Most of you dance like kings when you have big numbers. But when you have small numbers, you want to make the whole world feel bad. "I'm hurting. I don't have money." Grow up. It's hard to ask people to believe in you when you don't even believe in yourself.

Rise up! Stand up! You always have a chance. Things can change tomorrow. We're in business to change. And we're in business to win. Any army, any team, at the most crucial time, when you're down, when you hit the bottom, and you call the right shot, you rise up, the hero rises up, and you change the whole game! In the battlefield or the playing field, when it's the darkest of hours, at the weakest point, somebody rises up and changes the whole thing because somebody believed in himself and believed in the destiny of the team!

Chi Hsing-tzu was training
fighting cocks for the king.
After ten days the king
asked if they were ready.
"Not yet. They're too haughty
and rely on their nerve."
Another ten days passed
and the king asked again.
"Not yet. They still respond
to noises and movements."
After another ten days
the king asked again.
"Not yet. They still look
around fiercely and are
full of spirit."
Yet another ten days and
the king asked again.
"They're close enough.
Another cock can crow and
they show no sign of excitement. Look at them from a
distance and you'd think they
were made of wood. Their
virtue is complete.
No cocks are their match—
enemies will at once turn
and run."

— CHUANG-TZU

ANATOMY OF AN EXPLOSION

CONDITIONS FOR IGNITION:

1. A High Level of Frustration

2. An Unsual Surge in the Attitude of Leaders

3. A Big Dream Written Down in a Specific Plan

4. A Mastermind Alliance of Key Leaders

5. A Daring Action / A Bold Move

WINNING

Happiness

is helping

a friend become

financially

independent.

TAKE CHARGE OF YOUR BUSINESS

"God gets you to the plate, but once you're there, you're on your own."

– TED WILLIAMS

It puzzles me that there are so many dependent people who want to be financially independent. They never seem to know anything. Their favorite words are "Where?" "How?" and "Why?"

Many of these people have been in the business a long time, yet they act as if they joined yesterday. They look like the husband who goes into the kitchen and keeps asking his wife, "Where are the forks? How do I turn on the stove? Why won't the dishwasher work?"

> "Where is the class?
> Where are the forms?
> Where is the school?
> Where is the meeting?"
> "How do I recruit? How do I sell? How do I use the computer?"
> "Why won't anybody teach me? Why didn't anybody tell me? Why does this happen?"

When they go to conventions, they always let the upline book the room, rent the car, chauffeur them around, and even wake them up. A leader once said, "My business is running a giant adult day care!" Everybody admittedly laughed. Ironically, when these same people go on their own vacation, they plan and do everything—buy tickets, book the room, and rent the car—without any problem.

"It's a shame to be in a business of personal growth and never grow up!"

How can you ever become a leader if you keep letting people take care of you, remind you, and motivate you all the time?

Why don't you book your own room, rent your own car, and find your own way? Why don't you take charge of your business? Why don't you step up and become a servant leader?

It's not your upline's business. It's not your downline's business. It's not your sideline's business. It's not the company's business. It's your business.

One day, a team member asked me to teach him the features of a new product. My reply: "We are both licensed. We are both business people. This is a new product. How can you expect me to learn and teach you? Here is the brochure, the prospectus, and the forms. I have to read, learn, and understand the same product for my business. never expect anybody to learn for me. Why don't you do the same for your business?"

"You need to be independent before you achieve financial independence."

THE FEAR FACTOR

So many people let fear control them, hold them back, and slow them down.

WHEN THEY GO INTO BUSINESS, THEY EXPRESS SO MANY FEARS

* Fear of what people say
* Fear of rejection
* Fear of not knowing enough
* Fear of the competition
* Fear of failure
* Fear of speaking in public
* Fear of the uncertain
* And a lot more

> *"Fear is a luxury of your mind*
> *that you cannot afford."*

Fear Is Not Necessarily Bad, Actually It Can Be a Great Asset

REMEMBER ALL THE GOOD FEARS THAT YOU HAD?

* Fear of losing that fired you up in sports competitions
* Fear of disappointing your parents that helped you excel in class and attain good grades
* Fear of losing your job that keeps you working so hard
* Fear of ill health that motivates you to exercise and maintain a healthy diet

> *"Control your fear and turn it into good use."*

I used to fear all the negative things people could say, but then I realized that I would only prove them right if I listened to them.

I used to fear rejection. It killed me when people said No. But if I stopped, I feared I'd lose my next super-star, because I know I'm one recruit away from a big explosion.

I used to fear not knowing enough. I didn't want to be embarassed. But the fear of depending on other trainers, and not being able to learn fast, was more pressing.

> *"If I keep sitting in the passenger seat,*
>
> *I will never know the way."*

I used to fear the competition, but the fear of losing to them and missing the opportunity of a lifetime made me stronger everyday.

I used to fear failure, but the fact of going back to my job was even more daunting. That kept me going until I became successsful.

I used to fear speaking before crowds, but the fear of disappointing the team was even worse.

> *"I have so many fears in my life, but the biggest fear*
>
> *is being average and ordinary."*

We live with fear all our lives. Either we control fear, or fear will control us.

THE FOUR KNOWS

"Know your enemy and know yourself.
You can fight a hundred battles and win
a hundred of them."

— SUN TZU

1. KNOW WHAT YOU WANT

◆ Know the reason you go into business. What difference can you make in your loved ones' lives? Your spouse's, your kids', your parents', and others'?

◆ Have a clear goal. How much money do you want to make? How soon will you be financially independent?

◆ Have a well-thought-out plan. How wide-deep-big do you want your team to be?

> **HAVE A SPECIFIC GOAL, AT A SPECIFIC TIME**
> Imagine if a travel agent asks you where and when you want to travel, and your answer is: "Any destination is okay and any time is fine with me."
> It's your life. Be specific.

2. KNOWLEDGE

◆ Know the concepts, products, and services well

◆ Understand and run the system

- Recruit, build, and motivate
- Know your people
- Know your clients

3. KNOW YOURSELF

- Do you have what it takes to win?

- Know your weaknesses—e.g., procrastination, shyness, fear of rejection—and conquer them.

- Know your strengths—e.g., positive attitude, mental toughness, perseverance—and improve them.

- Know the price you have to pay, the sacrifices you're willing to make, in order for you to win.

4. KNOW THAT YOU'RE GOING TO WIN

- If you don't, you might as well quit right now.

"It's your business to know."

30 DAYS RELENTLESS

"Never go home before 11 PM."

The day I totally changed my life... it didn't come the first month, and it didn't come the second month. About 5 to 6 months in the business, the day I was so sick and tired of being a loser, I made a mental decision that I would never go home every night before 11 p.m.

That was the toughest discipline call I made in my life. Every night, I was out in the field, whether I had appointments or not. I was out there and I was not going home. That's why I drove around and around, and that's how I learned to drop by a prospect's or a team member's house. I would just stop by and talk business.

> Can you be in business for 30 days straight?
>
> Can you stay out in the field until 11 PM?
>
> Can you be relentless and inevitable?

Every night, I went out in the field. The first month was tough, but by the second month I was so busy because I had so many appointments. The first few weeks I had no appointments, but as I stopped by and dropped by enough people's homes, and as they gave me more leads and went out in the field with me, the activity I created snowballed and became unstoppable.

I made sure I was out in the field every night. And I would never go home before 11 o'clock. I just figured out that anyone who has a business is going to open their business every day. So I just did what a normal businessperson did.

You're not for real until you can pass this test. When working for someone else, most of us have no problem going to work everyday. But when we go to work for ourselves, we can't do it. When we're in business for ourselves, when we're our own boss, when we can do anything we want, we end up doing nothing.

A large majority of people cannot go out in the field even once a week! A handful can go out a few days a week. But only a chosen few can be out there everyday.

In our business quite a few people who go out in the field every night for 4 hours end up making more money than people who work 8 hours every day at their job.

JUST DO IT

When your team does not move,

keep on moving yourself.

If your team does not recruit,

you recruit.

If your team does not sell,

you sell.

If your team does not go to the meetings,

you go to the meetings.

If your team does not go to the convention,

this is the reason for you to go.

You care for your team.

But you don't care.

You need them.

But you don't need them.

Just keep on keeping on.

THE WISDOM TO WIN

"How high is your IQ? How smart are you?
How much do you know?"

Nowadays, we live in a world of information. There are thousands of newspapers, journals, newsletters, e-mail, and magazines, hundreds of TV channels, a zillion bits of information on the web at our fingertips, not to mention books, tapes, and radio. In addition to all these massive doses of information, we spend many years of our life in school and college.

Yet with all this education and information, does it mean that people nowadays are more knowledge-able? Knowledge doesn't mean knowing everything, but rather knowing some things well.

Does it mean that we are wiser? Despite all this education and information, there are bigger debts, smaller savings, and more bankruptcies than ever before. Technology is so advanced, yet more people work longer hours. The 40-hour work week will soon become a dinosaur. Currently, one half of families have two paychecks. This will soon become three quarters. Will this mean more traffic, more stress, more financial traps, and more divorce?

And yet we encounter so many people who are so impressed by themselves, by their degrees, their position, and their knowledge.

"Information does not necessarily create knowledge.

Knowledge does not necessarily create wisdom."

Are you knowledgeable enough and wise enough to become a builder? Can your brain bring you financial independence? Can you work with people? Can you build people? Can you use your ability to do what is necessary to win?

When people come to the business, they face the same challenges. They make the same mistakes. Instead of focusing on doing what is necessary to win—following the system and being coachable to the trainer—they're trapped in technical details of products, licensing, and researching. They spend days on the web, weeks reading brochures, months taking licenses. They end up with lots of information and knowledge about products—but nothing else!

> *"Don't have too much book sense.*
>
> *Have common sense.*
>
> *It's not what you know.*
>
> *What you do with what you know is the key."*

Ultimately, you must win. Focus all your strength and ability on making things happen rather than on watching what's happening.

THE KUNG FU MASTER

Once upon a time in China, high up in the mountains, there lived the greatest kung fu master of the time. Martial arts students all over the land came to learn from him. They worked hard, practiced day and night, and went through great sacrifices and pain. Many of them became famous and successful.

One day, a monk stopped by to visit him and asked, "Master, you produce so many successful disciples. Your reputation has spread all over. You should be very proud and happy, yet you seem to be sad and unsettled."

The master replied, "Sir, all my life, I trained thousands of students. I found most of them are good. The majority of them learn to be the fastest, strongest, and most powerful fighters. They come down the mountain to become generals, officials, and great martial artists. Some remember me and pay me a visit to offer gifts and thanks. They learned every-thing from me—except they don't want to do what I do. Not one wants to come up here and replace me!"

இ

TOO BUSY FOR YOUR DREAM

"You get busy all your life and then die."

The number one cause of failure in our business is lack of time.

"I don't have time," "I can't make it," "I have to work overtime," "I have a wedding to go to," "There's a party," "I have to pick up one of my relatives," "I'll be ready next month," "When I come back from the trip, I'll do it," et cetera, et cetera.

They show up to the office and disappear for a few weeks. They undergo licensing but can't finish. They want to go out to the field but can only do it once or twice. The minute they have some recruits, something always happens, and they can't work with them. Something always happens at the wrong time.

People are busy. They really are. I was one of them. Both my wife and I had full-time jobs. My job was quite demanding, so was my wife's. Between work, taking kids to school, picking them up, preparing dinner, and doing household chores, we were a very busy couple.

But that was just the beginning. There was always something to do, somewhere to go. We drove our kids to school meetings, baseball practice, swimming lessons, piano lessons, and karate lessons during the week. And during the weekends, we'd have to prepare for a party, or go to somebody else's party, or call someone to apologize for being unable to make it to their party. We went to birthday parties for kids, for adults, for friends, for in-laws. We celebrated baptisms, communions, weddings, anniversaries, graduations. We bought gifts for Father's Day, Mother's Day, Valentine's Day, Christmas, New Year's. We barbequed for every Laker game, Super Bowl, and World Series.

Everybody invites everybody, and everybody is afraid to say No because we're afraid that when the time comes for us to throw a party, our kid's birthday, our BBQ, people won't have time for us. When we go to a party, we talk about the people who don't show up.

"It's a system whereby parties never stop!"

Then Monday morning comes. We go to work to pay our bills. Christmas arrives. One year passes by. Every year, the next year seems busier than the last. We turn 40, we turn 50, we turn 60, and then we're too old. Now we stay home alone because our kids and grandkids are too busy going to their parties, weddings, and barbeques.

With all this time on our hands, we get to watch TV. We turn on the Travel Channel to see all the wonderful places in the world that we weren't able to go to because we didn't have the time or the money.

Welcome to the busiest place in the world. I walked down this busy street half of my life and finally woke up the day I saw the business presentation. I was fortunate because I was able to change. I didn't want to go through the rat race, running around like a chicken without a head. I wanted my life back.

Unfortunately, most people are not that lucky. They can't wake up. They can't get out. They can't change.

They have all the time in the world for their boss, their friends, their in-laws, and everybody else. But they never have time for their business. They're too busy for their dreams.

Almost everybody has no time. A handful shows up sometimes. Fewer people work part-time (at least 20 hrs/week, 4 hrs/day). And of course, very few become full time or go ballistic all the time.

> **WE HAVE 5 TYPES OF PEOPLE IN OUR BUSINESS:**
> 1. The No-timer
> 2. The Sometimer
> 3. The Part-timer
> 4. The Full-timer
> 5. The All-the-timer

♦ You can never do anything in life if you don't have time.

♦ You will definitely fail if you do things sometimes.

♦ You make some money if you work part-time.

♦ You make good money if you invest your full-time.

♦ But if you want to make a fortune, you must put your heart, your mind, and your effort into the business all the time.

"Either you follow other people's schedules
or you follow your own schedule.
Either you do it for you or you do it for others,
but you certainly will be busy."

SOMETHING TO BELIEVE IN

So many people do things they don't really believe in. Millions of people wake up in the morning, commute to work, and show up at a job they don't really believe in. They don't see their future there. They report to a manager they don't really believe in either. They're not sure their boss takes the best interests of them and their family at heart. They go to lunch with their coworkers and have some casual conversations. They go home and watch TV while life passes them by. They love their family and their children, but they're uncertain whether the children will be successful because they're not successful.

For me personally I came to a point in my life where I found that I had to make a decision. I went though that routine, the job, the situation with my family, and I told myself, if there's something I should do right now, I have to find something that I totally believe in and put my life into it. And the reason I am here is because I absolutely believe in what I do.

ℭℛ

FAMILY BUSINESS

We cannot make a difference for families until we help our family first.

Over the years we find that having the family involved turned out to be the most incredible thing to happen to our family and to our lives. I don't think the work is the issue. But to be able to have the family help the family business and help other people have brought us together.

I don't know about other families, but ever since I joined this business and I involved my family I never had to explain what I do. When I travel long distance, and many days I'm not home, I tell my wife, when the kids ask where I am, you have two choices. You can say dad is going to work, or you can say dad is going out to do good things for our family and for other families. The first answer is a separation of family and business, the second makes business and family as one.

The bottom line is we do everything for ourselves and our family, and the main reason we are here is because we're doing something good for our family. Our mission is to make a difference for families. And this should be clear from the beginning.

Why is that so easy to understand when we go to work at a job? Our spouse supports it. Our children know it. What about this business? The family needs to give the same support here as with a job.

CR

HELPING PEOPLE

"To give pleasure to a single heart
by a single act is
better than a thousand heads
bowing in prayer."

— GANDHI

I grew up during the war. I saw desperate situations everywhere. All the temples and the churches were packed with people, so were the refugee camps and military bases.

In our business, we pack our meetings and conventions with people. We talk about our crusade, our mission to help people. But how sincere are we about what we do?

How desperate are people out there for an opportunity? How badly do they need help for their financial survival?

Even still, there is so little action, so few appointments. So keep praying.

There are so many people who say they want to help but they hardly move. In fact, they can't even help themselves. They don't recruit, they have no sales, they make no money, and yet they say they want to lead and impact others.

THE SIX-FIGURE TRAPS

"The invisible limitations."

What they said when they started does not matter. The goals they declared last year do not matter. How much they said they love the team does not matter. How much they said they want to help people does not matter.

What they said in the past carries no weight. It's their actions that speak the loudest.

Most people, intentionally or unintentionally, slow down mentally first and physically after as soon as they hit a six-figure income.

◆ When they hit 100K, a large majority of newly promoted MDs get trapped. They're too busy working in their business, opening their own office and maintaining the base.

> **BUILDER'S NOTE:** Most of these people don't realize that once they slow down, their 100K, 250K, or 500K income is not going to maintain either. "There are some strange farmers in some strange land who grow a farm in the first few years but neglect them after that and expect it continue to grow and bear good crops forever."

- When they hit 250K, some pass the first level, building a few more MDs and expanding to a few more locations until they hit this income.

- When they hit 500K, very few move on. Very few keep building and expanding. They build good superbases, and the hierarchy starts growing. But they become distracted. They look for a new house and new cars. They no longer go out in the field. They'd rather motivate other people to do that. Their spouse no longer engages in the business like before. They hope the new leaders do their job. After all, it's their chance to enjoy the fruits of their labor.

Sometimes I wonder whether someone will move on to seven figures?

"Success has ruined many a man."

— BEN FRANKLIN

WHAT DO YOU MAKE?

1. Make a living
2. Make good money
3. Make a fortune
4. Make a difference
5. Make history

"At what level will you stop or slow down?"

MOST PEOPLE WON'T STAY

"If you're not so sure if you will stay or not,
why expect people to stay?"

Quitting is one of the main characteristics of our business. Don't be so surprised! In fact, I'd be surprised if you are surprised about it.

If people have a choice, human nature dictates that they normally will quit.

In our business, people won't stay. They think they have nothing to lose when quitting. If they go to work, they can't quit. They have to pay the bills. If they spend a few hundred thousand dollars to buy a business, they won't quit either. The bottom line is whether they have to or don't have to.

"Most people know that they have
nothing to lose when quitting, but what they don't
know is that they lose a lot."

I remember every semester when I went to
night school for adult continuing education. The classes
were packed at the beginning of the semester.
It was even difficult to find a parking space. But after
1 or 2 months, the classes were half empty.
And by the end of the semester, I'd drive into a deserted
parking lot. Every 6 months, the same thing happens.
On the other hand, the college never had this
quitting problem for daytime students.

QUIT WITHIN THE FIRST 72 HOURS

Within the first 3 days, they talk to 10 to 20 of their friends and relatives. Guess what they're going to hear? All the negative things in the world. Most can't survive the first round of attack.

QUIT WITHIN THE FIRST 30 DAYS

These people are a little stronger than the first group. They do PPL, BMP, and invite. But people say No to them, jack them around, stand them up. Finally, they recruit one or two people. But unfortunately their recruit quits, so they quit too.

QUIT WITHIN THE FIRST YEAR

A handful stay. They recruit some people, get licensed, and begin to go out in the field. They make a few sales once in a while and go to meetings and conventions occasionally. They like the business but find it too tough. Many people don't buy from them. Their team is not committed. Their spouses don't give them support. Little by little, it will kill them.

YOU'RE NOT FOR REAL UNTIL YOU LAST MORE THAN 18 MONTHS

Everything in life, the starting period is always very tough. Whether you open a restaurant, start a real estate brokerage, become a freelance artist, or launch a financial services career, the first 1 to 2 years are survival time, even if you try hard.

But if you hang on for the first 18 months, you may survive and have a long term commitment for the business.

There is no miracle here. This is not a get-rich-quick scheme. You must want it bad. You must work hard. You must give your business total commitment.

"What about your job?
Does it get you anywhere in the first 18 months?"

IT TAKES AT LEAST 5 YEARS TO BUILD A GOOD BUSINESS

MY FIRST 2 YEARS: SURVIVAL

* Prospected, invited a lot; few came

* Recruited some but they didn't last; didn't listen, didn't go to the meeting, didn't get licensed, didn't sell if they got licensed

* Learned to drop by, recruit, sell, and earn some money

"The best thing I learned
was not to be killed by all the bullets that are
shot at me everyday."

MY NEXT 2 YEARS: WORK, WORK, WORK

* Became full time

* Became a good producer and a good trainer

* Built a habit of discipline

* Earned a six-figure income

* Learned to follow the system

* Began to have a vision

* Developed a strong passion for the mission

* Started building the base

MY 5TH YEAR: BECAME A SYSTEM BUILDER

*   Built a strong baseshop
*   Built a strong foundation for base thru 1st
*   Understood the system and the business
*   Built long distance
*   Organized meetings and big events
*   Became confident about my recruiting mentality, builder's mindset, meeting mentality, and leading by example
*   Developed winning habits
*   Became a major earner
*   Stayed on track to my dream

"Yes, you can do it if you stay!"

JUST WANT TO BE ME

"About 19 years ago, I no longer wanted to be
a good husband. I just wanted to be me."

I grew up in a poor family. My dad died when I was
16. My mother never worked outside of the home.
My brothers and I had to work at an early age to
support our large family.

I always wanted to be a good kid. I went to work
and school at the same time. Every penny I
earned, I gave to my mother, so she could have
money to take care of expenses. Not only did I
work hard at work, I worked hard to excel in
school, so that my mom would be proud of me.
Even after I got married, whatever money I could
save I would send to my mom.

There were many times when I wanted to do
things for myself–buy something, travel somewhere… But I set it aside, hoping that one day I
would be able to do it. I constantly felt ashamed
that I couldn't do more for my family. I looked at
others who were richer than me, who were able
to do more for their families than me. That killed
me inside.

I always wanted to be a good husband. After I got
married, I wanted to do so much for my wife. But I
was a poor social worker. My income was limited.
I also lacked many skills of a typical husband.
Looking at people around me, not only could they

afford great things for their wives, they also knew how to fix the car, tend to the garden, build the deck, and hook up the computer. As for me, I'm terrible at those things. Everything I touched, I messed up. The more I tried to be a good husband, the more frustrated I became. I was in a losing game.

I always wanted to be a good father. Then I had children. Whenever I read books on how to be a good father, I felt so small. I looked at all good husbands on TV shows, and I felt ashamed. I couldn't afford things for my kids. I wasn't good at teaching them sports. I spent my time doing birthday parties and driving my kids around, but I wished I could be a better father.

I always wanted to be a good son-in-law. I wanted my wife's family to be proud of me. So no matter how busy I was, I would set aside time to do good things for my in-laws.

I always wanted to be a good friend, a good employee, and a good relative. I always wanted to make people happy and feel good about me. Although there were times when I had financial challenges, as well as life challenges, I always put those people ahead of me.

When I reached the age of 36, I was a miserable man. I was poor. My job was insecure. My future was bleak. I spent all my life trying to make people happy, but I myself was unhappy. I did not feel good about myself.

Then, one Saturday morning, I saw the BPM. That changed my life. I was so excited about the business opportunity. But I didn't know what to do between a full-time job, a family, a brand new business opportunity, and making everyone else happy.

I made a tough decision: I no longer wanted to be a good husband, a good father, a good son, a good son-in-law, or a good friend.

I just wanted to be me. I decided to stop making others happy and finally decided I just wanted to do things that made me happy.

I closed my eyes, plugged my ears, and moved forward, going after my dream. I did not fulfill much of my role as a husband. I let my wife take care of the children. I stopped hanging around my friends. Negativity spread all over. People told me I was crazy. They told me I was too much into money. They said that I wouldn't last too long.

But I endured, I made money, and I won. It was a long, tough fight, but it changed my life forever. After the first year in the business, I doubled my income. After the second year, I tripled it. By the third year, I made a six-figure income and retired my wife. I kept building a big team and a successful business. I became financially independent.

I found out an important thing. Before, I spent my life trying to make other people happy, but I was broke and unhappy. In reality, though, I wasn't able to help anybody, and they weren't so happy either.

Now, I spend my life for me. I live my dream every day. I am truly happy. But even better, I also can make my family's dreams come true. My wife doesn't need to go to work, and I am able to provide for my children and help people around me.

When I travel, I hear the flight attendant say, "Put on your oxygen mask first, before you help your children or others." I agree with that advice.

"It's hard to help others
when you're unable to help yourself.
It's hard to make others happy
when you're unhappy."

HANDWRITTEN SIGN FOUND ON THE WALL OF MOTHER TERESA'S ROOM

- *People are often unreasonable, illogical, and self-centered; forgive them anyway.*

- *If you are kind, people may accuse you of selfish, ulterior motives; be kind anyway.*

- *If you are successful, you will win some false friends, and some true enemies; be successful anyway.*

- *If you are honest and frank, people may cheat you; be honest and frank anyway.*

- *What you spend years building, someone could destroy overnight; build anyway.*

- *If you find serenity and happiness, others may be jealous; be happy anyway.*

- *The good you do today, people will forget tomorrow; do good anyway.*

- *Give the world the best you have, and it may never be enough; give your best anyway.*

- *For you see, in the final analysis, it is between you and God. It was never between you and them anyway.*

Make a Wish

Have a Dream

See the Vision

Live the Mission

Follow the System

Build a Team

Be SomeBody

– XUAN NGUYEN
System Builder